{LIT 'n' LaTTes}

Adding Faith and Fun to Your Book Club

Loveland, Colorado
group.com/women

Group

Lit 'n' Lattes: Adding Faith and Fun to Your Book Club
Copyright © 2009 Group Publishing, Inc.

Visit our Web site: **group.com/women**

Credits
The Well-Read Wonders Who Wrote This Book: Dana Bail, Pam Clifford, Janna Firestone, Helen Goody, Kate Holburn, Candace McMahan, Lori Poppinga, Beth Robinson, Ann Marie Rozum, Jill Wuellner
Executive Developer and Literary Lovely: Amy Nappa
Chief Creative Officer: Joani "Toss Me a Magazine" Schultz
Art Director (and Most Creative Scribbler): Andrea Filer
Copy Editor and "Bookaholic": Julia Wallace
Print Production Artist: YaYe Design
Cover Designer: Andrea Filer
Illustrator: Andrea Filer
Production Manager: DeAnne "Chick Lit" Lear

Unless otherwise indicated, all Scripture quotations are taken from the *Holy Bible*, New Living Translation, copyright © 1996, 2004. Used by permission of Tyndale House Publishers, Inc., Carol Stream, Illinois 60188. All rights reserved.

Library of Congress Cataloging-in-Publication Data
Lit 'n' lattes : adding faith and fun to your book club.
    p. cm.
 ISBN 978-0-7644-3714-4 (pbk. : alk. paper)
1. Book clubs (Discussion groups) 2. Christians—Books and reading.
3. Women--Books and reading. 4. Cookery.
 LC6619.L58 2008
 367--dc22
                         2008027516
10 9 8 7 6 5 4 3 2 1   18 17 16 15 14 13 12 11 10 09
Printed in the United States of America.

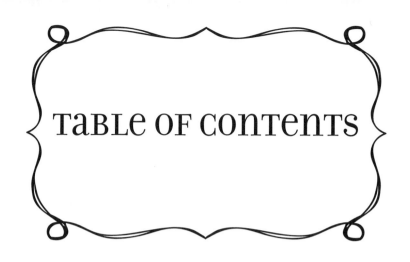

TABLE OF CONTENTS

HELLO,
MY FELLOW reader!

I've always been a reader...proudly getting a library card as soon as I was old enough, sneaking Nancy Drew titles under the covers with me at night (and then wondering why I had nightmares about people sneaking out of trap doors in my closet), and dragging sacks of books along on vacations. My dad would read aloud to us after dinner every night, laughing through *Pippi Longstocking*, giving us goose bumps as we followed the adventures of Bilbo Baggins, or leading us in cheering on our favorite Narnian heroes.

My nightstand is still crowded with books (I usually have two or three going at the same time), and I often carry them around the house, stirring food in the kitchen with one hand while holding a book in the other, or pretending I'm watching football with my husband when I'm really engrossed in a thriller.

A few years back, one of my sisters invited me to a book club that she'd recently joined. We read and discussed *A Very Long Engagement* (which is very long...but also very engaging!) and I was hooked. What fun to gather with a bunch of women once a month, dig into the heart of interesting literature, and eat yummy treats as well! I was challenged to read books I might never have picked up on my own, found new treasures, discovered authors that I wished I could have coffee with, and made incredible friends in the process. And, interestingly enough, I also grew in my faith! So many books, even if they weren't written by Christian authors, had messages of redemption, growth, and enduring love—things I could relate to my relationship with Jesus.

And that's where this book comes in. Perhaps you'd like to start a book club (after all, it's a great excuse to get together with girlfriends!). Or maybe your book club needs some fresh ideas. Or it could be that you want to draw more spiritual truths from the books you're reading. This book is for you!

{Cracking the Spine of *Lit 'n' Lattes*}

Lit 'n' Lattes features 24 books with enough variety to appeal to all kinds of women. We have stories to make you laugh and some that will make you cry. Classic literature as well as newer reads. You'll find thrillers, dramas, romances, and even a bit of time travel.

The titles featured in this book were chosen because women love them and they can encourage great spiritual discussions. That said, a book's inclusion here doesn't mean we endorse all of the content in that book. **Note: You should always read a book yourself before recommending it to your book club. Only you can judge the type of material that is appropriate for your group, so please make sure you read it before recommending it.**

Each book includes a short summary of the plot (without spoiling the ending) and some info on why women will enjoy it. You'll also find suggestions for a snack, dessert, or other food idea that ties to the theme or characters in the book, ideas for adding pizazz through decorations, invitations, or gifts for your guests, plus relevant discussion questions and Scripture passages that relate to the themes of the story.

Book Club Basics!

- Be sure you've read the book first before recommending it.
- Gather girlfriends who like to read. You can create a *Lit 'n' Lattes* group that meets monthly to read and discuss books. See if women want to take turns hosting, or if perhaps you and a friend want to share the hosting and discussion-leading.

- Prep by reading the ideas provided in *Lit 'n' Lattes* that correspond to the book you've chosen and selecting the ones you want to use.
- Pray that God will use the time together to deepen friendships and to help women draw closer to Jesus.
- When everyone arrives, welcome them with coffee or tea and delicious treats and get everyone chatting.
- Relax and have fun!

The discussion questions dig into the heart of the content of each book, and will help women both get to know each other better and also explore the spiritual themes of the book. Even if a book was not written by a Christian author, there are spiritual messages to be found in each of the ones we've included.

{Basic Discussion Questions}

For each book the suggested questions are very specific to that book. Here are a few questions that will work with *any* title— you might want to use one or two of these to get your discussion started before digging into the meatier questions.

- Which character can you relate to most and why?

- What were the key themes of this book?

- Which events in this book touched you in a surprising way?

- Has this book changed your opinions about anything? If so, what?

Ready to get reading? Head to the library or a local bookstore and start turning those pages!

Amy Nappa

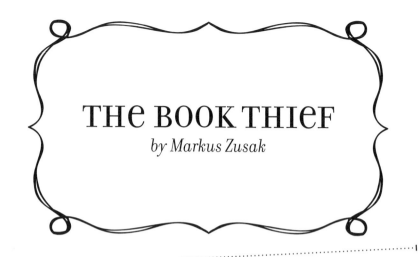

THE BOOK THIEF
by Markus Zusak

{Book Review}

The Book Thief tells the story of Liesel, a young girl growing up near Munich, Germany, during the time of Adolf Hitler. Raised by non-Nazi foster parents on the poor side of town, Liesel treasures books and the new worlds opened to her by them. Unfortunately, the poverty of her family means there's only one way for Liesel to get books—by stealing them. The story is told from the point of view of the angel of death, who gives us a personalized account of Liesel's life.

{Critic's Comments}

This is a story filled with both joy and sadness, and the reality of what can happen when you reach out to help others. Women will be drawn to the heartwarming love shown by Liesel's adopted family, as well as the redemption found even in pain. And the quirky point of view expressed by the narrator adds a unique touch to this story.

Note: This is the account of a family dealing with war; there are German curse words translated into English and nongraphic wartime violence.

{A Novel Treat}

I···

... German Vanilla Kipferl Cookies

Liesel and Rudy make a trip a few weeks after Christmas to 8 Grande Strasse for just one more book. This time, there are leftover Christmas cookies awaiting them; and the realization that the open window is a window of opportunity.

___2 cups all-purpose flour

___1 cup (3½ ounces) natural sliced almonds

___pinch of salt

___1 cup (2 sticks) unsalted butter, at cool room temperature

___¾ cup confectioner's sugar

___½ vanilla bean, split lengthwise

___1 large egg yolk, or more as needed

Vanilla Sugar

___½ cup granulated sugar

___½ vanilla bean

Cookies

Use a food processor to grind flour, almonds, and salt until almost a powder. With a heavy-duty mixer, beat butter until smooth (about one minute). On low speed, slowly beat in confectioner's sugar; then return to high speed and cream together until mixture is very light in color and texture (about two minutes), scraping sides of the bowl frequently. With a small sharp knife, split the vanilla bean lengthwise; scrape out seeds and pith; add to creamed butter and sugar mixture; reserve pod. Add egg yolk and blend together. Using a spoon, blend in flour mixture until dough is stiff and holds together when pressed. (If dough is crumbly, add another beaten egg yolk.) Remove dough from bowl and form into a thick disk shape; wrap in plastic and refrigerate for at least one hour. Note: You can do this up to two days ahead.

Preheat oven to 350 degrees. Line baking sheets with parchment paper.

Spoon out two teaspoons of dough, and roll it between your hands to soften; it will be crumbly at first, but keep rolling. Roll into a 3-inch rope with tapered ends. Shape rope into a crescent and place on baking sheet.

Bake for 15-17 minutes, until cookies are a light golden brown around the edges. Cool for two minutes on baking sheet and remove to wire rack. While cookies are still warm, pick up gently and dust in vanilla sugar.

Vanilla Sugar

In blender, process sugar, vanilla bean, and reserved vanilla pod until the bean is very finely chopped and the sugar is ground into powder. Use a sieve to sift out the larger pieces of vanilla. Set aside for sprinkling on cookies later.

Makes about 50 crescent-shaped cookies.

{Quotes from *The Book Thief*}

"Before they went into their respective homes, Rudy stopped a moment and said, 'Goodbye, *Saumensch*.' He laughed. 'Good night, book thief.'

It was the first time Liesel had been branded with her title, and she couldn't hide the fact that she liked it very much. As we're both aware, she'd stolen books previously, but in late October 1941, it became official. That night, Liesel Meminger truly became the book thief."

"She tore a page from the book and ripped it in half.

Then a chapter.

Soon, there was nothing but scraps of words littered between her legs and all around her. The words. Why did they have to exist? Without them, there wouldn't be any of this. Without words, the *Führer* was nothing. There would be no limping prisoners, no need for consolation or wordly tricks to make us feel better.

What good were the words?

She said it audibly now, to the orange-lit room. 'What good are the words?'"

That's Interesting!

According to the author, Markus Zusak, "This is an unforgettable story about the ability of books to feed the soul." Zusak's mother lived in a small German town. As a child, he heard his mother's stories of Jews being marched through her town, and of Nazi Germany, and the bombing of Munich. Hearing these stories, he knew this was a story he wanted to tell.

{Pizazz}

Ration cards were a big part of German life during WWII. Families bartered with rationed items to get things they needed to survive. Use the illustration below to create your own German ration cards as invitations to your book club.

{Cracking the Spine}

Use these questions and comments to get women talking:

- Books meant a lot to Liesel; so much that she was willing to steal them. Describe how books impacted your life as a young teen. What impact do they have on your life today?

- Liesel and the Hubermanns lived on Himmel Street. The translation for Himmel is *heaven*. Why do you think the author chose this name for this street?

- Growing up, most of us heard stories of Nazi Germany and assumed everyone in Germany supported Hitler. *The Book Thief* shows us a different side of Germany and those who rebelled against Hitler's

 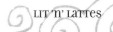

regime. Have you ever thought about what it was like for these people? How do you think you would respond if something like this happened in your own country? Would you take similar risks?

- Thievery is a big part of life for the young people in Molching. Sometimes they stole to feed themselves or provide gifts for loved ones. What would bring you to the point of you stealing?

- Ephesians 4:28 says, "If you are a thief, quit stealing. Instead, use your hands for good hard work, and then give generously to others in need." Describe how you think God would feel about the stealing Liesel and Rudy did. Also consider, what was being stolen from *them*?

- Matthew 25:40 talks about feeding "the least of these brothers of mine" (New International Version). Describe Hans Hubermann's reaction to the Jews marching through his neighborhood, and compare that to the message in this verse.

{The Reference Section}

You may want to use these additional Bible verses during your discussion.

- Matthew 9:36—The compassion of Jesus.

- Ephesians 4:32—Be kind to others.

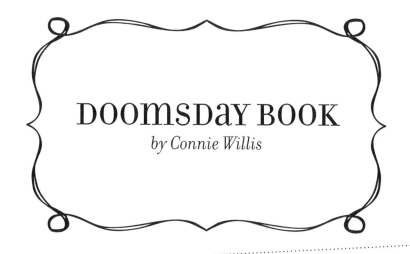

DOOMSDAY BOOK
by Connie Willis

{Book Review}

The year is 2054 and time travel is now reality. Kivrin, a student at Oxford, is being sent to the 1300s, the time of the 100 Year War, the Crusades, and the Black Plague. Unfortunately, an epidemic hits London just as she leaves, and no one knows exactly what year she landed in or where she is. Did she avoid the Black Plague, or land right in the middle of it? Will her mentor, Mr. Dunworthy, be able to find her and bring her back to the present? *Doomsday Book* takes a parallel track as readers follow both past and present stories in this imaginative book.

{Critic's Comments}

With a strong heroine and a fast-moving story that mixes humor, drama, prejudice, and compassion, women will find *Doomsday Book* both fun and fascinating. This is a book that creatively examines questions we all have about human nature and God. *Where is God when bad things happen? Why does God allow suffering? Is God really in control?* You're sure to have a great discussion!

{A Novel Treat}

... Oatmeal Cookies

With the epidemic and rationing in London, Colin wasn't so excited about a breakfast of oatmeal. If Finch had been thinking, these oatmeal cookies might have been a better treat for the guests staying at Balliol.

____1 cup margarine or butter, softened

____1 cup packed brown sugar

____½ cup granulated sugar

____2 eggs

____1 teaspoon vanilla

____1½ cups all-purpose flour

____1 teaspoon baking soda

____1 teaspoon cinnamon

____½ teaspoon salt

____3 cups quick or old-fashioned oats

____1 cup of raisins or chocolate chips

Preheat the oven to 350.

In a large bowl, combine the margarine and sugars. Beat until creamy. Add the eggs and vanilla, beating well.

In another bowl, combine the flour, baking soda, cinnamon, and salt. Add to the sugar mix, and stir until all ingredients are combined. Stir in the raisins or chocolate chips, mixing well.

Drop by tablespoonfuls onto an ungreased cookie sheet. Bake 10 to 12 minutes or until golden brown. Cool 1 minute on the cookie sheet and then remove to a wire rack.

Makes about 4 dozen.

{Quotes from *Doomsday Book*}

A conversation between Roche and Kivrin:

"I feared that God would forsake us utterly, but in His great mercy He did not, but sent His saint unto us."

"And I'm no use."

"Why do you weep?"

"You saved my life, and I can't save yours."

"All men must die, and none, nor even Christ, can save them. Yet have you saved me. From fear. And unbelief."

{Pizazz}

Despite the name, this is a great book to read during the Christmas season. And if you're one who enjoys decking the halls, this will be a fun book for which to decorate. Kivrin, Agnes, Rosemund, and Roche all go to gather ivy and holly for decorating the house. Even if you don't live in a climate where these grow naturally, they're easily accessible at any craft store. Gather some to place on your mantle, countertop, tables, and so on. Along with the greenery, use candles to add ambiance, and if you have a fireplace, burn a Yule log.

That's Interesting!

- *The Domesday Book* was actually a land survey taken in 1086 by William the Conqueror. While it didn't include everyone living in England at the time, the census was so extensive it was later called the "Doomsday Book" in reference to the Book of Life mentioned in the Bible during the Last Judgement.
- Connie Willis is a Christian.
- The character Mr. Dunworthy also appears in Willis' 1998 time travel novel *To Say Nothing of the Dog*.

{Cracking the Spine}

Use these questions and comments to get women talking.

- If you could travel to a different time, where would you go and why?

- In the story, Imeyne despises Roche and is critical of everything he does, while upholding the drunken bishop and his clerk. How did this story challenge your prejudices? Tell about a time someone's behavior positively changed your opinion that was based on an outward appearance.

- Discuss some of the parallels between the story taking place in the 1300s and the story taking place in 2025 (the bells, the epidemic, characters with similar personalities). How did these reinforce the themes the author was examining?

- Kivrin was placed in a situation for which she was emotionally unprepared. Read 2 Corinthians 12:9 and tell about a time you had to do something you felt was beyond your ability. How did you see God's hand working in and/or through you?

- When Kivrin is alone at the end of the book and talking into the corder, she says to Mr. Dunworthy, "It's strange. When I couldn't find the drop and the plague came, you seemed so far away I would not ever be able to find you again. But I know now that you were here all along, and that nothing, not the Black Death nor seven hundred years, nor death nor things to come nor any other creature could ever separate me from your caring and concern. It was with me every minute." Read Romans 8:38-39. How does Kivrin's experience compare to this passage?

- How is Mr. Dunworthy's relationship with Kivrin like God the Father's relationship to Christ? How are they dissimilar?

{The Reference Section}

You may want to use these additional Bible verses during your discussion.

- Lamentations 3:22-23, 31-32—God's mercy and compassion.

- Romans 8:38—The unfailing love of God.

ELLa Minnow Pea

by Mark Dunn

{Book Review}

Ella Minnow Pea is a delightful story set on the fictional island of Nollop, named after Nevin Nollop, who (according to the story) created the phrase "The quick brown fox jumps over the lazy dog." This memorable sentence that contains all the letters of the alphabet is sacred to the people of Nollop.

When the letters on the memorial honoring Nollop's phrase begin to fall off, those letters are banned from use on the island. This "novel in letters" then becomes a linguistic challenge, both to this grapheme-based society and to the reader. The result is a clever and hilarious story with a profound satirical statement on censorship, tyranny, and the art of letter writing.

{Critic's Comments}

Ella Minnow Pea has a sense of charm about it. Even though it's set in contemporary times, the Victorian letter-writing style and small-town demeanor of the citizens of Nollop depict a simpler, more innocent lifestyle. The ridiculous laws add whimsy and satire to the plot, creating a more complex scenario and making the book appealing both as a lighthearted read and a literary experience for word lovers. *Ella Minnow Pea* lends itself to a great discussion on faith versus cultural convictions.

{A Novel Treat}

... Aunt Mittie's Zesty Grapheme Soup

___2 cans alphabet soup

___one 9-ounce package of fresh tortellini

___1 can of black beans

___one 9-ounce package of refrigerated salsa (in the grocery store's deli section)

___fresh cilantro (optional)

___low-fat sour cream or plain yogurt (optional)

Mix the soup, tortellini, beans, and salsa in a saucepan. If the soup is condensed, add water according to the directions. Simmer at medium heat for about 15 to 20 minutes, or until tortellini is tender.

Serve in mugs with a dollop of sour cream and a sprinkling of fresh chopped cilantro. Serves 4 to 6.

Add to the fun of your gathering by seeing what words women can spell with the letters in their mugs!

{Quotes from *Ella Minnow Pea*}

"The devils aren't in Japan! The devils are here. Satan is alive and well, right here in all his z-q-j-d-k-f-b, jumpy-brown-fox-slothful-pooch-quick-and-the-dead-glory—right here upon this devil's island of hatred and anger and unconscionable, inconsolable loss." (Amos)

"In the disquieting quiet, we wonder and worry, yet try to carry on some semblance of normal life." (Ella)

{Pizazz}

If you have a Scrabble game you're willing to part with, glue some of the letter tiles onto cards to make invitations. Or cut letters from empty cardboard cereal boxes and glue them on cards for invitations. Inside, try writing your invitation lipogram-style. Here's an example of one that avoids the letter E:

"Join in on book club fun! Jot down your book thoughts and bring 'um along. Slow down. Chill out. Chomp on good food. Laugh a bit with your gal pals! And catch a bit of God!"

Write the day of the week using one of the alternative choices in the book such as "Monty," "Wetty," or "Thurby."

That's Interesting!

- If you have the hardcover version of this book, the subtitle is *A Progressively Lipogram-matic Epistolary Fable*. The later-released softcover is subtitled *A Novel in Letters*.
- "The quick brown fox jumps over the lazy dog," is a *pangram*—a sentence that uses all the letters of the alphabet at least once. Another pangram is "How quickly daft jumping zebras vex."
- A lipogram is a constrained style of writing, where the author deliberately avoids the use of certain letters of the alphabet. Here are some well-known works of literature created lipogram-style:

Gadsby by Ernest Vincent Wright (1939)—missing the letter E

Eunoia by Christian Bök—each chapter is missing four of the five vowels

Gyles Brandreth rewrote some of Shakespeare's more famous plays:

Hamlet—without the letter I ("To be or not to be, that's the query")

Macbeth without letters A or E

Twelfth Night without letters O or L

Othello without the letter O

Episodes of *The Simpsons* and *Gilmore Girls* have also delved into lipogrammatic dialogue.

{Cracking the Spine}

Use these questions and comments to get women talking.

- It's clear that some of the characters have issues with "worshipping" Nevin Nollop as a false god rather than respecting and honoring him as a historic figure. What's the difference between worship and respect? How do characters in the story resolve this conflict? How do you resolve this in your own life?

- Do you think the citizens of Nollop are conflicted with faith issues, or conflicted with having to set aside their faith for law? Have you ever overlooked your faith in Jesus for a cultural conviction?

- Do you think Georgeanne was correct to report Mittie's slip of the tongue? How does this novel comment on the conflict of respecting and questioning authority?

- How does the Office of High Island Council try to use logic to define "Nollopian" religion? How do they disregard logic? How might logic either interfere with or strengthen your faith?

- How does this novel comment on the complacency of American society?

- As a letter-based society, how are the people culturally challenged at the loss of losing letters? How is that like having faith without leaning on Scripture?

- Read 1 Timothy 1:3-7. Compare this passage to the themes of the book.

{The Reference Section}

You may want to use these additional Bible verses during your discussion.

- Exodus 20:3-4—Idol worship.

- Philippians 1:9-11—Living by God's grace.

The Great Divorce
by C.S. Lewis

{Book Review}

Lewis' allegorical classic centers around a dream journey through the realms of the afterlife. The narrator takes an extraordinary bus ride on which he encounters residents of both Heaven and Hell and visits astonishing spiritual worlds. With George MacDonald as guide to this bizarre-but-wonderful adventure, the narrator encounters truths that will transform his (and the reader's) life.

{Critic's Comments}

This haunting and fantastical adventure will guide women's minds to contemplation and their hearts to meditation. They'll discover God's extraordinary grace and realize the profound importance of each everyday choice.

{A Novel Treat}

... Light and Dark Cookies

Serve dually-frosted cookies as a tangible symbol of the contrast between spiritual lightness and darkness, Heaven and Hell. You'll need sugar cookies, white frosting, and chocolate frosting (as dark as possible).

Make life a little easier by picking up pre-made containers of frosting from the grocery store. If you opt for homemade cookies instead of store-bought, follow this recipe.

___¾ teaspoon baking powder

___3 cups flour

___¼ teaspoon salt

___1 cup unsalted butter, softened

___1 cup sugar

___1 egg (beaten)

___1 tablespoon milk

___powdered sugar

Sift together baking powder, flour, and salt. Using an electric mixer, beat butter and sugar until the mixture is a light color. After adding milk and egg, beat again. Keeping the mixer on a low speed, gradually add the baking powder, flour, and salt. Beat until the dough comes away from the sides of the bowl. For best results, refrigerate the dough for a couple hours. When you're ready to bake, preheat your oven to 375 degrees.

Sprinkle flour or powdered sugar over the surface where you'll roll out the dough. Also sprinkle flour or sugar over your rolling pin. Roll out dough to one-quarter-inch thick, handling it as little as possible so that it stays cool. Cut the dough into circles, and place about one inch apart on a greased baking sheet. Bake about 9 minutes, rotating the cookie sheet halfway through baking time. You'll know they're ready when they start to turn slightly brown around the edges. Remove from oven and cool. Frost half of each cookie with white frosting and half with chocolate frosting.

Makes about three-dozen small cookies.

{Quotes from *The Great Divorce*}

"'There are only two kinds of people in the end: those who say to God, "Thy will be done," and those to whom God says, in the end, "Thy will be done."'" (George MacDonald)

"If we insist on keeping Hell (or even earth) we shall not see Heaven: if we accept Heaven we shall not be able to retain even the smallest and most intimate souvenirs of Hell." (Lewis)

"And still the light grew."

{Pizazz}

Colors, and their underlying symbolism, play a big role in this story. Consider decorating your room to fit this theme. Adorn half the room in dull, drab tones such as gray and off-white; then garnish the other half with vivid, beautiful color. Use throw pillows, sheets (to cover furniture and tables), streamers, and flowers.

Or, since much of the story takes place on a bus, you might set up your room to resemble a bus. Create two parallel rows of seats with an aisle in between, and suspend sheets or blankets from above to create a "roof."

That's Interesting!

This work inspired several musical endeavors, including: James Clapperton's string quartet piece "The Great Divorce" off the album *The Cold Dancer: Contemporary String Quartets from Scotland;* Phil Woodward's entire album *Ghosts and Spirits,* and Caedmon's Call's song "The High Countries" from the album *Back Home.* Consider purchasing these pieces online and playing them quietly in the background.

{Cracking the Spine}

Use these questions and comments to get women talking.

- This book focuses on an amazing journey. How do you view your own faith journey? What comparisons and contrasts can you make to the narrator's?

- Do you have a friendship with someone you consider to be a spiritual guide? If so, what have you learned from this person? What is the value and impact of people like George?

- How do you imagine heaven? When you think of heaven, what do you feel? Excited, nervous, uncertain, terrified, confused? Explain.

- How do Lewis' portrayals of heaven and hell change your view of an afterlife? How does this affect your relationship with God? with others?

- In the story, things of heaven are painful to hell-bound phantoms. Why is this meaningful? When are things of God painful to those who reject a relationship with God?

- What does this book reveal about the power of God's grace? How would you describe what God's grace means to you in one sentence? What about joy?

{The Reference Section }

You may want to use these additional Bible verses during your discussion.

- Ephesians 1:13—We belong to Christ.

- 1 Peter 1:8-12—The joy of salvation.

- Hebrews 11:16—Heaven.

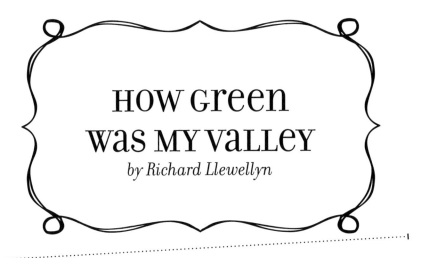

HOW Green was MY valley

by Richard Llewellyn

{Book Review}

The story "begins at the end" as narrator Huw Morgan packs his things to leave home forever, and it unfolds as he reminisces about his youth, his loved ones, and a valley once green and vibrant with life.

We follow Huw as he grows from a small boy to a young man in a Welsh coal mining region, but this is more than just his own coming-of-age story. Like the slag heap from the mines that encroaches upon Huw's town, dark issues of vigilante justice, hypocrisy, thwarted love, industrialization, and workers' strikes threaten to bury the once idyllic life of everyone in the Valley. But all is not grim in Huw's world—Llewellyn's lyrical prose describes a life that is also brightened by family loyalties, first loves, and priceless friendships. By the end of the novel, we grieve along with Huw for the passing of a time when his Valley was green, "and the Valley of them that have gone."

{Critic's Comments}

As women, we feel that we know these characters. In stirring, poetic language, the narrator shares the lives of people dear to him—and by the end of the book, they are dearly loved by us.

{A Novel Treat}

… Blackberry Tarts from Mama

To encourage Huw's recovery after he rescued her from drowning, Mama brought him a blackberry tart "with such a taste that will make you close your eyes and wish you might live for ever in the wideness of that rich moment." Share a rich moment with your guests when you serve these easy pastries.

Filling:

____4 cups fresh or frozen blackberries

____½ cup sugar

Wash fresh berries or defrost frozen ones. Sprinkle with sugar and set aside while you prepare the pastry shells.

Pastry shell:

____3 cups flour

____1 cup shortening

____7-8 tablespoons water

Preheat oven to 350 degrees. Sift flour and salt then cut in the shortening. Add water a little at a time, cutting mixture until crumbly. Shape dough into two balls, then roll each to about ¼-inch thickness. Cut circles out of the dough big enough to line muffin pans and lightly press the dough into each pan. Fill with blackberries and bake for 35 minutes or until each tart shell is lightly browned.

Makes 18 to 24 tarts.

30

{Quotes from *How Green Was My Valley*}

"You know your Bible too well and life too little...Let there be moderation in all things, Saint Paul said, and a more sensible man never trod the earth." (Mr. Gruffydd)

"Yet Conscience is a nobleman, the best in us, and a friend." (Huw)

{Pizazz}

As a memento of the valley, surprise your guests with lavender sachets like the kind Bronwen made for her sheets and her wash.

For each sachet, cut a circle about 4 inches in diameter from an old white handkerchief, pillowcase, or other lightweight cotton fabric. Place a spoonful of lavender buds (sold at most health-food stores) into the center of the circle, then fold up the outer edges of the circle and gather with string or narrow ribbon.

Placed on the dash of a car or in a drawer, these sachets will remind your guests of their "journey" to a Welsh valley of long ago—and of their group of book-loving friends!

That's Interesting!

Richard Llewellyn took twelve years to write *How Green Was My Valley,* writing and rewriting as he researched his material by working in a Welsh coal mine. When it was published, no one had heard of the new author—but his book was an instant success and, in 1941, was voted "Bookseller's Favorite Fiction" in America. Producer John Ford made the novel into a movie that won Best Picture that same year.

{Cracking the Spine}

Use these questions and comments to get women talking.

- Do you think the Morgan sons honored their father and their mother by their actions? Why or why not? Give examples.

- Ianto accused a visiting preacher of doing "useless work" as the shepherd of a flock that lived in filth and poverty. On the other hand, Mr. Gruffydd agitated some people by his involvement in the politics of the region. Which do think is a more appropriate stance for men in their positions? Why?

- Do you think Huw's love for Ceinwen differed from his love for Bronwen? If so, how would you explain different types of romantic love?

- Romans 14:13 says, "So let's stop condemning each other. Decide instead to live in such a way that you will not cause another believer to stumble and fall." How can we relate this verse to Mr. Gruffydd's response when the town gossiped about him and Angharad? Have you ever had to sacrifice something you loved (for example: a hobby, a job, or a friend) in order to appease others? Share your experience.

- Huw believed that "women have their own braveries, their own mighty courageousness that is of woman, and not to be compared with the courage shown by man." Who did you feel was the most courageous woman in this story? Why? Tell about a brave woman you know.

- For their last Bible reading before the family was separated forever, Dada chose Isaiah 55:1, "Come, all you who are thirsty, come to the waters; and you who have no money, come, buy and eat! Come, buy wine and milk without money and without cost" (translated from King James). Why do you think he selected this particular verse?

- How did events within this story affect Huw's faith? His mother's? How can we reconcile with the fact that bad things still happen to people who love God?

{The Reference Section }

You may want to use these additional Bible verses during your discussion.

- Exodus 20:12—Honor your parents.

- Proverbs 3:5-6—Trust in God.

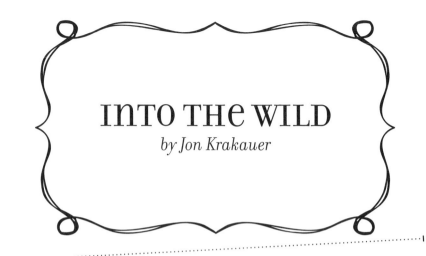

INTO THE WILD
by Jon Krakauer

{Book Review}

This is the true story about the life and death of Christopher McCandless, a restless young man discontent with the comfortable lifestyle most people would wish for. Upon college graduation, McCandless donated his life savings to charity, packed only what was necessary for a bare-minimum survival, and followed the credo to go west. Throughout his years on the open road he touched many lives, but refused any meaningful relationships that would interrupt his vagabond travels.

McCandless' journey became headlines when his stubborn intent to live solely off the land in primitive Alaska took a disastrous turn. Krakauer reassembles the facts around McCandless' short life, compelling readers to ask themselves if he took his resolve too far.

{Critic's Comments}

Jon Krakauer's writing brings outdoor adventure into our living rooms. Even the less adventurous won't be able to resist peeling back the curtain for a sneak peek into the journey of a young man with a reckless, daring spirit.

Note: There are occurrences of profanity in excerpts from McCandless' letters and journal entries.

{A Novel Treat}

... Travelers' Gorp Balls

Rather than foraging for wild berries like Christopher did, we think your guests will enjoy munching on these tasty, nutritious snacks—favorites with hikers and travelers:

___⅓ cup each dried chopped apples, apricots, shredded coconut, raisins or dates, and walnuts

___2 cups peanuts

___½ cup sesame seeds

___1 cup chocolate chips

___½ cup peanut butter

___⅓ cup honey

In large bowl combine all the dry ingredients. Stir in the honey and peanut butter (this will act as the glue). Shape into bite-size balls and serve.

Makes about 24 balls.

{Quotes from *Into the Wild*}

"You are wrong if you think Joy emanates only or principally from human relationships. God has placed it all around us. It is in everything and anything we might experience. We just have to have the courage to turn against our habitual lifestyle and engage in unconventional living." (McCandless)

"It is easy, when you are young, to believe that what you desire is no less than what you deserve. To assume that if you want something badly enough, it is your God-given right to have it." (Krakauer)

{Pizazz}

Print your favorite quote from the book and attach it to a small packet of Fireweed flower seeds. As your guests leave, present them with these mementos so they can enjoy the same flowers that surrounded Fairbanks Bus 142.

That's Interesting!

Like McCandless, Jon Krakauer headed into uncharted Alaskan territory as a young man. When he was 23 years old he quit a construction job in Colorado and traveled into the Northwest to climb the face of the Devils Thumb, a mountainside no man had yet traversed. His story ends more favorably than McCandless, but he compares his experience (which he shares in the book) as a raw youth mistaking passion for insight with that of McCandless'.

LIT 'N' LATTES

{Cracking the Spine}

Use these questions and comments to get women talking.

- Do you think McCandless was cocky or confident in undertaking his journey? Explain.

- When Krakauer's original article ran in *Outdoor Magazine*, Alaskan residents were hard on McCandless, saying he lacked the necessary humility to observe, ask questions, and think to survive in the wild. Would you agree that he held an insufficient respect for the land? Why or why not?

- If you picked up McCandless for a ride and he told you his plans for walking into the wild, what would you say to him?

- What do you think of McCandless' decision to walk away from his identity and past life without a glance in the rearview mirror? Could you do the same? Would you discuss your plan with your family and friends, even if you knew they would try to discourage you?

- Krakauer believes that McCandless was bitter about his discoveries concerning his father's past. How do you think his resentment may have influenced his expedition? Have you ever been influenced by resentment? If so, how?

- It seems to be man's innate nature to be the hero, conquer adversity, seek adventure, and explore the unknown. How do you think this plays into McCandless' story?

- Thousands of years ago, another notable young man set out on a journey of self-discovery. He walked away from the comfortable surroundings of his friends and family, and, led by the Holy Spirit, he walked into the desert alone with no food or water for 40 days and 40 nights. What, if any, comparisons can you draw from McCandless' journey with that of Christ's?

{The Reference Section}

You may want to use these additional Bible verses during your discussion.

- 2 Corinthians 4:18—The temporary versus the eternal.

- Mark 8:34-37—The cost of following Jesus.

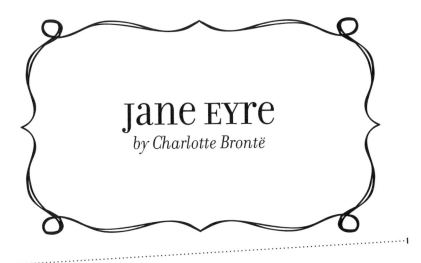

jane Eyre
by Charlotte Brontë

{Book Review}

Jane's young life seems empty and hopeless until a series of events leads her through boarding school and ultimately to a post as governess at Thornfield Hall. There she meets—and falls secretly in love with—the master of the household, Mr. Rochester. But strictures of Victorian England don't promote romantic liaisons between governesses and their employers—and what's more: Jane is not exactly considered a "catch." Mr. Rochester, on the other hand, is arresting in looks, demeanor, and financial status.

Does his interest in Jane suggest a mutual attraction? Or does he have dark, ulterior motives? After all, he's hoarding a secret of his own—but his is rather gruesome…

{Critic's Comments}

Not just another romance, this novel broke the mildewed mold of nineteenth-century "chick lit" and it's been a classic favorite ever since. The heroine is plain, not glam; spirited, not passive; and intellectually witty, not vapid. With a brave and spirited heroine, a tempestuous hero with a mysterious past, and plenty of stormy relationships set amid a gothic backdrop in the moors of England, this story meets every requirement for the perfect fireside (or beachside) read.

{A Novel Treat}

... St. John's Scones

Mary and Diana Rivers served Jane "little cakes" while she rested at Moor House. Their recipe was likely similar to this one, and it's surprisingly simple (no kneading, rolling, or cutting). Best served with tea, of course!

___2 cups flour

___⅓ cup sugar

___2 teaspoons baking powder

___¼ teaspoon salt

___6 tablespoons cold butter, cut up

___½ cup milk

___1 large egg

___⅓ cup raisins, cranberries, or currents (optional)

Heat oven to 425 and grease two cookie sheets.

Mix the first four dry ingredients in a large bowl, then cut in butter with a fork until the mixture is crumbly. In a separate bowl, beat milk and egg together. Add to flour and stir until moistened, then gently fold berries into the mix.

Drop 12 heaping spoonfuls onto cookie sheets, keeping dough 2 inches apart. Don't worry about "forming" the scones. If desired, lightly sprinkle with additional sugar.

Bake for 13 minutes or until golden. Cool on a rack (but also good served warm).

Serves 12.

{Quotes from *Jane Eyre*}

"You are a strange child, Miss Jane...A little roving, solitary thing..." (Bessie)

"I thought there were excellent materials in him; though for the present they hung together somewhat spoiled and tangled." (Jane)

{Pizazz}

Transport your guests to Victorian England with a few simple touches. If you don't already own one, beg, borrow, or buy a teapot with cups and saucers (is there a thrift store near you?) and complete the mood with flowers—lots of flowers. Roses, lavender, or sprays of heather will summon images of estate parlors or cozy English cottages.

That's Interesting!

Though diminutive in size (a preserved dress of hers could probably fit an 11-year-old), Charlotte Brontë was a giant among literary talents, especially those who were women. But because her style of writing (and that of her sisters') was considered bold for its time, she and her sisters originally wrote under masculine pen names so their work would be taken seriously.

{Cracking the Spine}

Use these questions and comments to get women talking.

- Which of Jane's qualities did you most appreciate—her intelligence, her dry wit, her loyalties, her artistic abilities, or her inner strength? Why? What are the good qualities you saw in Jane that you see reflected in those around you in the room right now? Name a positive quality for each person.

- Imagine that you've traveled in time to Victorian England. With the skills set that you currently have, how might you have supported yourself? How would that era have suited you? disagreed with you?

- Throughout the novel, Jane is on a quest for love and a sense of belonging. What were her obstacles? Would she have encountered the same struggles if her story took place today? Explain.

- Mr. Brocklehurst, Helen Burns, and St. John Rivers were each passionate about religion. How did they differ from each other in their perceptions of God? How did their faith differ from Jane's? Can our individual concepts of God affect the way we treat other people? Explain.

- If you were Jane, how would you have reacted when Mr. Rochester revealed his secret? Did he, as he defended, have a right to "deliver" himself from his marriage to a mentally ill woman? Why or why not?

- In John 14:27, Jesus said, "I am leaving you with a gift—peace of mind and heart. And the peace I give is a gift the world cannot give. So don't be troubled or afraid." How does this verse relate to Jane's prayer experience when she left Thornfield Hall and was overcome by fears? What happened after she changed her prayers to those of thanksgiving? Have you ever felt an instant peace by thinking about God's power? Please share.

- There was so much more to Jane than most people bothered to see. What strengths or characteristics do you have that others aren't aware of? Be honest! Now's the time to brag a little!

{The Reference Section }

You may want to use these additional Bible verses during your discussion.

- 1 Peter 3:3-4—Unfading beauty.

- 2 Corinthians 2:5-11—Forgiving others.

THE MEADOW
by James Galvin

{Book Review}

This is a tale of two families—the Worsters and the Van Wanings—and their lives on a ranch near the Wyoming-Colorado border over a span of nearly 100 years. In the face of six-month winters, isolation, and unremitting toil, they build their homes and their lives. It's a story of a vanishing way of life in which self-sufficiency goes hand in hand with friendship, and mental and physical toughness live side by side with tenderness. It's a story about a place of almost mythical beauty and harshness and how it shapes the character of those who live there.

{Critic's Comments}

If you were born or raised in the rural West, you'll find that this book describes the deepest, most enduring parts of that heritage. If you're simply interested in the Western way of life, you'll be fascinated by its complexities and seeming contradictions. If you stand in awe of God's creation, this book will tap into feelings you may not know you possess. Finally, if you just love breathtakingly beautiful writing, you'll cherish this book.

Note: This book does contain occasional profanity.

{A Novel Treat}

... Clara's Oatmeal Cookies

Nothing tastes better on a cold, snowy day than these old-fashioned oatmeal cookies, straight from the oven, accompanied by a glass of milk or a hot cup of coffee.

___1 cup shortening

___1 cup sugar

___1 cup brown sugar

___2 eggs

___3 cups rolled oats

___1½ cups flour

___2 heaping teaspoons baking soda*

___½ teaspoon salt

___1 teaspoon vanilla

___1 cup chopped walnuts or pecans (optional)

*If doubling the recipe, use 3 heaping teaspoons baking soda.

In a large bowl, mix shortening and sugars until well blended. Add eggs and mix well. Add rolled oats, flour, baking soda, and salt. When well blended, add vanilla. If desired, stir in walnuts or pecans. Refrigerate 1 hour, then drop spoonfuls of batter onto a non-greased baking sheet.

Bake at 325 degrees for 10 to 12 minutes.

Makes 3 dozen cookies.

Note: This recipe is not good with raisins.

{Quotes from *The Meadow*}

"By the end he had nothing, as if loss were a fire in which he was purified again and again, until he wasn't a ghost anymore."

"You need a bad winter to have a good year."

{Pizazz}

Some livestock brands have been in the same families for generations and are just as much a part of their identities as their family names.

Design a brand for your book club, and reproduce it on the front of your invitation. You can find examples by searching on the Internet for cattle brands. Your group might like your "brand" so much that they decide to use it indefinitely!

That's Interesting!

James Galvin is a poet who didn't intend to publish *The Meadow*, his first book of prose. Rather, he wrote the book for his daughter, Emily. He said the book was his "attempt at saving memories, a lifestyle I was watching disappear in front of my eyes." First published in 1992, *The Meadow* remains Galvin's most popular work.

{Cracking the Spine}

Use these questions and comments to get women talking.

- Galvin writes, "A man who likes solitude doesn't necessarily like loneliness." What's the difference between solitude and loneliness?

- In the book's opening poem, Robert Duncan writes, "Often I am permitted to return to a meadow…that is mine, it is so near to the heart." Is there a place like this—even if it's not a meadow—in your heart? If so, tell about that place.

- Think about Lyle's conversations with the various missionaries who made the long trek to his home. What answers would you be prepared to give to Lyle's questions?

- James Galvin wrote *The Meadow* for his young daughter. What important things do you want your children to know about your life and your values that they may not already know?

- Clay rode horseback 15 miles in a blizzard to invite Lyle to Christmas dinner, even though he knew Lyle would refuse the invitation. How do you interpret Clay's effort and Lyle's response?

- Compare Lyle's words and actions with those of his neighbor, Earl Ferris, in light of Luke 6:45: "A good person produces good things from the treasury of a good heart, and an evil person produces evil things from the treasury of an evil heart. What you say flows from what is in your heart."

{The Reference Section}

You may want to use these additional Bible verses during your discussion.

- Psalm 8:3-8—The beauty of creation.

- Job 12:7-10—Learning from what God has created.

peace LIKe a RIver
by Leif Enger

{Book Review}

Eleven-year-old Reuben Land recounts his family's quest to find his prodigal brother, Davy. Beginning with the circumstances of his birth, Reuben is often the sole witness to bona fide miracles performed by his genuine and humble father. When the family packs up for the incredible journey to find Davy, the circumstances seem beyond miraculous. Where will God lead them? Who will they meet along the way? Will they find Davy?

{Critic's Comments}

Coupled with western heroes, romance, and adventure, this book displays a consistent theme of faith. Readers follow a dedicated father and three children through joyous, uncertain, and tragic times. This book is an inspiration of family love, religious faith, and the lifelong work and trust required of both.

Note: This book includes the subject of murder and a brief incident of implied abuse.

{A Novel Treat}

... Baked Oatmeal Buffet

The Lands' tradition was to begin the day with a hot bowl of oatmeal. Whatever toppings were available in the cupboard were used to make each bowl special. Whether you choose to meet with your book group for a morning brunch or an evening, serve this treat and be sure to encourage others to bring a favorite topping.

____1 cup butter, melted

____2 cups brown sugar

____4 eggs, beaten

____4 cups old fashioned rolled oats (not quick serve)

____4 teaspoons baking powder

____2 teaspoons salt

____2 cups milk

Mix the ingredients together. Pour into a greased 9x13 baking dish. Bake at 350 degrees for 30 minutes. Cool for 15 minutes and spoon out to serve. Serves 12.

Note: The oatmeal can be made ahead of time. After cooling, store in plastic bags in the refrigerator. Reheat individual servings or larger portions in the microwave.

Suggested toppings:

Toasted coconut	Assorted fresh fruit	Walnuts
Granulated sugar	Cream	Pecans
Brown sugar	Butter	
Assorted dried fruit	Maple syrup	

{Quotes from *Peace Like a River*}

"You can't hurt what you can't find." (Reuben)

"Fair is whatever God wants to do." (Reuben)

{Pizazz}

To make your gathering unforgettable, provide each woman with a road-trip survival kit. Be creative and include fun items such as a snack, a personal fan or heat pack (depending on the season), a map, a notepad with a pen, and a potpourri sachet. Or, to create more involvement in your group, treat this as a gift exchange. Ask each woman to bring an item she never leaves home without and exchange these gifts.

That's Interesting!

- While touring for the book, the author brought his wife and boys along for the traveling. They enjoyed long drives, people, and the time together as a family. In one stretch, they drove 10,000 miles in 31 days.

- Asthma is a key problem in this story. Currently, 6.8 million children suffer from this condition.

{Cracking the Spine}

Use these questions and comments to get women talking.

- When Leif Enger had barely begun writing the book, one of his boys came into the office asking if there were any cowboys in the book. Enger replied, "No, not yet. But that's a fabulous idea. You think I should?" After a resounding Yes, Leif asked his son for a good name. His son said, "Sunny Sundown," with no hesitation. By the end of the day the first few stanzas of "Sunny" were written. How have children unexpectedly inspired you in your life?

- After Davy was arrested, Reuben recounts both the kindness of complete strangers and letters sent to Davy in prison, while "a lot of people we did know, and whose cheerful encouragement I'll bet Dad could've used, were staying away." When have you seen a situation like this in your own life? Why do you think it happens? Discuss the impact friends can make during difficult times.

- Jeremiah Land regularly studied his Bible and "held to it like a rope ladder." Compare this description to 1 Thessalonians 2:13, "Therefore, we never stop thanking God that when you received his message from us, you didn't think of our words as mere human ideas. You accepted what we said as the very word of God—which, of course, it is. And this word continues to work in you who believe."

- After Reuben received $25 for tearing down Mr. Layton's corncrib, Reuben decided to spend the money on groceries for Christmas instead of the canoe he desired. If you could spend $25 on something just for you, what would it be? Now share a time when someone made a sacrifice for you.

- Reuben first describes Roxanna as kind yet lacking beauty. As they spend time together, he then describes her as one of the most beautiful women he knows. Define *beauty* by describing the most beautiful woman in your life.

- Swede cherished the handmade saddle she received from Davy, though she didn't have a horse to ride. Tell about a thoughtful gift you have received.

{The Reference Section }

You may want to use these additional Bible verses during your discussion.

- John 15:13—The greatest love.

- Luke 15:11-32—The prodigal son.

MY SISTER'S KEEPER
by Jodi Picoult

{Book Review}

In this ripped-from-the-headlines novel, you'll feel the tug of both sides of the issues facing the Fitzgerald family. Thirteen-year-old Anna is suing her family for control over her own body. Anna's older sister, Kate, is dying; only Anna (or specifically, one of Anna's kidneys) can save her. Over the years, Anna has been subjected to numerous surgeries to help keep Kate alive, but this time it's different. By the time you arrive at the surprise ending, you'll feel so connected to each of the characters you'll find it hard to separate yourself from their story. Will you side with Anna? with Kate?

{Critic's Comments}

This book raises important ethical issues. We all think we'd do the right thing for our sister…but would we if it meant less of a life for us? Be aware you will share this family's intimate lives during a trying time, which can be very emotional.

Note: This book does contain profanity.

{A Novel Treat}

... Goldfish Clusters

Kate has wanted a pet forever. For her eighth birthday, her parents give her a pet goldfish, which she names Hercules and carries all around the party. These treats add gooey sweetness to a fish-shaped snack—your guests will love them!

___1 package (6.6 ounces) original-flavor Goldfish crackers

___½ cup extra-chunky peanut butter

___6 ounces semi-sweet chocolate chips

Place chocolate chips in a medium to large microwave-safe bowl and microwave on high until melted, stirring every 30 seconds. Add peanut butter for final 20 seconds and stir until combined.

Pour goldfish crackers into melted mixture and stir until well coated. Some crackers will break during the stirring, so be as gentle as possible. Drop by tablespoon onto waxed paper. Cool until firm (about 2 hours) and store in an air-tight container until served. Makes about 24 clusters.

{Quotes from *My Sister's Keeper*}

"Mr. Alexander, my sister has leukemia." (Anna)

"I'm sorry to hear that. But even if I were willing to litigate against God again, which I'm not, you can't bring a lawsuit on someone else's behalf." (Campbell Alexander)

"It's not God. Just my parents. I want to sue them for the rights to my own body." (Anna)

"Although I am nine months pregnant, although I have had plenty of time to dream, I have not really considered the specifics of this child. I have thought of this daughter only in terms of what she will be able to do for the daughter I already have." (Sara)

{Pizazz}

One theme running throughout *My Sister's Keeper* is the strong tie between sisters. When you're in a book group with girlfriends, that bond can become like that of sisters. An inexpensive gift idea that reinforces this thought is notecards you can make for each of your guests to take home.

Simply use your computer to create a card that says "A Sister Is Forever" in a pretty or whimsical font (you can download free fonts from the Internet). Print these onto colorful cardstock and fold in half to make notecards. Tie about 18 inches of ribbon around a set of six cards and color-coordinated envelopes, making one packet of cards for each of your guests.

There are real-life examples of siblings being conceived specifically as donors to older ill siblings. Children born for this purpose have been titled "Savior Siblings." Usually the older siblings have serious illnesses that they will die from unless they have an exact genetic match. Jodi Picoult chose the topic for this book based on the story of Katie Trebling and the Trebling family from Long Island, NY.

{Cracking the Spine}

Use these questions and comments to get women talking.

- What are your personal views on the moral and ethical issues raised in this book?

- In Genesis 22, God asks Abraham to sacrifice his son, Isaac. How does that compare with the Fitzgerald family's "sacrifice" of Anna's wellness to extend and possibly save Kate's life?

- The idea of conceiving a child to serve as a savior sibling could be described as playing God. While we don't all conceive children for this purpose, what are other ways we "play God" in our lives and in our children's lives?

- John 15:13 says, "There is no greater love than to lay down one's life for one's friends." How does this verse apply to Anna's desire not to donate her kidney to Kate…and threaten her own life? Have you ever *not* wanted to give up something that you knew would help someone? What happened?

- The phrase, "love your neighbor as yourself" is used throughout the Bible. Do you feel Anna is living this command? Why or why not?

- Anna and Kate's older brother, Jesse, is the problem child of the family. He has not had to sacrifice almost as much as either Kate or Anna because he wasn't sick like Kate or donation-worthy like Anna. How would you describe the meaning behind Jesse's behavior? How does that behavior impact the outcome of this story?

{The Reference Section }

You may want to use these additional Bible verses during your discussion.

- Luke 10:26-28—Love your neighbor as yourself.

- Matthew 19:19—Honor your parents.

THE Samurai's Garden

by Gail Tsukiyama

{Book Review}

Stephen, a young Chinese college student, becomes ill with tuberculosis in the years just before World War II. His parents send him to recuperate at his family's summer home in Japan, though China and Japan are already at war. At first, Stephen feels isolated and lonely. But over the course of a year, he comes to know Matsu, the caretaker and gardener; Sachi, a woman whose life is shrouded in mystery; Kenzo, a friend from Matsu's childhood; and Keiko, a beautiful Japanese girl with whom Stephen shares a tender romance. As the story unfolds, Stephen learns about belonging, love, devotion, and beauty.

{Critic's Comments}

The Samurai's Garden is a gentle, slowly unfolding story of devotion and love that remains constant over a lifetime of adversity. It's about people who find quiet beauty in the natural world, in the simplicity of daily routines, and in loving service to one another.

Note: This book is about non-Christian people in Japan. The characters participate in many Shinto and Buddhist rituals. While the characters pray, they do not pray to God. There is one affair, at least one romantic relationship outside of marriage, and one brief mention of a child conceived outside of wedlock. However, the language describing these events is not offensive.

{A Novel Treat}

... Udon Noodle Soup

Treat your guests to this tasty Japanese soup. You may also want to serve rice crackers and hot, unsweetened green tea. Rice crackers can be found either in the Asian section of your grocery store or in the gourmet cracker section.

____1 block of firm tofu

____3 tablespoons white miso paste

____1 cube fish or vegetable bouillon

____1 package Udon noodles

____a few handfuls of fresh baby spinach

Bring 2 quarts of water to a boil in a large pot. Put the miso paste in a small bowl. Add a small amount of boiling water and stir to dissolve. Add the dissolved miso into the large pot of boiling water. Add the bouillon cube and the Udon noodles. Boil for 5 minutes. Turn down the heat. Cut the tofu into bite-sized cubes. Add to the pot and warm through. Just before serving stir in several handfuls of fresh baby spinach. Serve with red chili paste if desired. This recipe will serve 8 people an appetizer-sized portion of soup.

Note: Miso paste comes in many varieties. White miso is very mild in flavor. If you prefer something more adventurous, try red miso. Miso and Udon noodles can be found in the Asian section of most grocery stores.

{Quotes from *The Samurai's Garden*}

"The garden is a world filled with secrets. Slowly, I see more each day. The black pines twist and turn to form graceful shapes, while the moss is a carpet of green that invites you to sit by the pond. Even the stone lanterns, which dimly light the way at night, allow you to see only so much. Matsu's garden whispers at you, never shouts; it leads you down a path hoping for more, as if everything is seen, yet hidden. There's a quiet beauty here I only hope I can capture on canvas."

{Pizazz}

Give an inexpensive packet of seeds or an inexpensive green plant, such as a small ivy or jade, to each of your guests as they leave. Type up the following paraphrase of Colossians 1:10 and print it on a decorative card using a flowery font to attach to each of the seed packets or plants:

"I pray that you'll live well for the Master, making him proud of you as you work hard in his garden. As you learn more and more how God works, you will learn how to do *your* work. I pray that you'll have the strength to stick it out over the long haul—not the grim strength of gritting your teeth but the glory-strength God gives."

That's Interesting!

- Gail Tsukiyama is interested in "people trying to persevere while living apart from society."

- Tsukiyama's father was a Japanese American, and her mother was Chinese. The kernel of inspiration for this book came from her uncle who had business connections in Japan just before World War II.

- *Samurai* is a term that refers to the military nobility of preindustrial Japan. The word is derived from an archaic Japanese verb, *samorau*, that means "to serve."

{Cracking the Spine}

Use these questions and comments to get women talking.

- Early in the book Stephen says, "It's harder than I imagined, to be alone." Many of the characters in the book lead lonely lives. How do the characters cope with loneliness and isolation? How do you deal with loneliness and isolation in your own life?

- How and why do the characters move from isolation and loneliness to interconnectedness and interdependence as the story unfolds?

- Throughout his life, Matsu nurtures a beautiful, lush garden of trees and colorful flowers, while Sachi tends a dry garden of stones. What is the significance of the gardens in this book? Why is the book titled *The **Samurai's** Garden*? Read Galatians 5:22-23. How is the metaphor of a garden also appropriate for Christians?

- The reader learns about several romances as the story unfolds. What lessons can you glean from the many romances that fail and the one that is constant? Why have Matsu and Sachi remained constant in their love for one another?

- Some of the characters in this book grow stronger despite (or because of) the loss and adversity they face. Other characters cannot face the difficulties in their lives. What is the difference in the way these individuals respond to loss and adversity?

- The themes of shame and honor are woven throughout this book. Tomoko and Kenzo deal with their shame through suicide and by doing so bring honor to their family. But Sachi cannot bring herself to end her life and withdraws to the mountains. As a believer in the grace and forgiveness that comes through Christ, how did reading about these methods of dealing with shame affect you?

- As the other characters come to know and trust Stephen, he learns intimate details about their lives. How does Stephen change as he learns more about others? How do the others change as they tell Stephen their stories? How do we change when we know one another's stories?

{The Reference Section }

You may want to use these additional Bible verses during your discussion.

- Galatians 6:9-10—Don't tire of doing good.

- Galatians 6:2—Carry each other's burdens.

THE SECRET LIFE OF BEES

by Sue Monk Kidd

{Book Review}

Lily Owens is a 14-year-old girl who lives with her abusive and neglectful father and her nanny, Rosaleen. Lily vaguely remembers her real mother and is unable to believe the stories her father tells about her. After finding a picture of a Black Madonna that belonged to her mother with "Tiburon, South Carolina" written on the back, Lily escapes from her home and ventures out with Rosaleen to find the truth. Lily and Rosaleen are taken in by three bee-keeping sisters. What they learn from these sisters and experience in their home is beyond imagination. What's so special about Tiburon, South Carolina? Will Lily find and be able to rest in the truth of her mother?

{Critic's Comments}

This book contains many themes including self-actualization, the search for significance, and how this all compares with the fascinating life of bees. Women will be touched by the relationships that develop and the longing to "belong."

Note: This book does contain instances of abuse, racial discrimination, and coarse language. Worship of the Virgin Mary is included as an element of this story and will provide a good discussion for your group.

{A Novel Treat}

… Sweet Potato Biscuits

May has incredible special needs and a huge heart. One of her specialties in the kitchen is Sweet Potato Biscuits. Prepare these ahead of time and serve them with butter, honey, and hot tea with assorted honey sticks.

___2 cups self-rising flour

___3 tablespoons brown sugar

___¼ teaspoon ground cinnamon

___⅛ teaspoon ground allspice

___¼ cup butter

___3 tablespoons shortening

___1 cup mashed sweet potatoes

___6 tablespoons milk

___2 tablespoons butter, melted

Combine flour, sugar, cinnamon, and allspice. Cut in ¼ cup butter and the shortening with a pastry blender until mixture is crumbly. Add mashed sweet potato and milk, stirring just until dry ingredients are moistened.

Turn dough out onto a floured surface and knead just a few times.

Roll dough out to ½-inch thickness; cut with a 2-inch biscuit cutter. Place biscuits on an ungreased baking sheet and brush with melted butter. Bake at 400 degrees for 12 minutes, or until browned. Makes 15-18 biscuits.

{Quotes from *The Secret Life of Bees*}

"I learned more from my grandmother than I did in the whole eighth grade." (Lily)

"Most people don't have any idea about all the complicated life going on inside a hive. Bees have a secret life we don't know anything about." (August)

{Pizazz}

Bees, honeycombs, and honey surround the lives of the three sisters. Carry this idea through by making a unique invitation for your book club. Decorate the invitation by stamping with shapes cut out of honeycomb sheets. Then tie a bow around a flavored honey stick and attach one to each invitation.

That's Interesting!

- It takes honeybee workers 10 million foraging trips to gather enough nectar to make one pound of honey.
- "A worker [bee] is just over a centimeter long and weighs only about sixty milligrams; nevertheless, she can fly with a load heavier than herself" (*The Honey Bee*).

{Cracking the Spine}

Use these questions and comments to get women talking.

- The sisters' beekeeping hobbies became their livelihood...from honey to honeycombs and candles to recipes. What are your hobbies? If you could learn a new hobby, what would it be?

- According to *Queen Must Die and Other Affairs of Bees and Men*, "Honeybees depend not only on physical contact with the colony, but also require its social companionship and support. Isolate a honeybee from her sisters and she will soon die". How do bees compare to women? Why is social companionship and support critical to our lives? What happens when you are cut off from other women?

- August shares, "Every bee has its role to play." Compare this statement to that of spiritual gifts found in 1 Corinthians 12:12-31.

- Secrets are critical to the plot of this story. How do you feel about keeping secrets? Is it better to get things out in the open or keep them hidden? Explain your perspective.

- Lily's entire quest surrounds the memory of her mother and needing closure to what she remembers and what others tell her. Why is a relationship with a mother so critical? Where does the burden for that relationship's strength lie—with the mother or with the daughter? Explain.

- The sisters and a few friends in the community comprised the Daughters of Mary, a religious group surrounding the wooden statue of Mary. Compare the practices of the Daughters of Mary with your own beliefs.

{The Reference Section}

You may want to use these additional Bible verses during your discussion.

- Deuteronomy 6:3—The land of milk and honey.

- Judges 14:14—Honey: part of Samson's riddle.

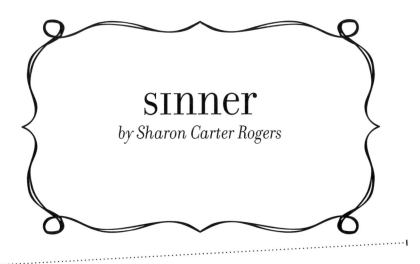

sinner
by Sharon Carter Rogers

{Book Review}

When a priest is brutally attacked in his church, the curiosity of author CK Ivors is piqued. And when a mysterious symbol, dating back to the Civil War, is found at the scene, nothing can keep her from investigating the crime. To many the symbol is just the mark of an urban legend, a superhero of sorts called the Sinner. But as CK begins to look into the past and interviews people who have seen the Sinner, she becomes convinced he's not just a myth.

Soon CK is tangled in a web of people also looking for the Sinner, and some of them don't play so nice. Will she solve the mystery before harm comes to her and others? Will the Sinner find rest for his soul?

{Critic's Comments}

Sinner delves into the question of God's forgiveness in a unique way that engages the reader on several levels. Women will enjoy the fact that the story's heroes are women, and while they're not perfect, they're smart and brave. While *Sinner* contains examples of man's brutality, it also holds illustrations of tender mercy and God's faithfulness toward those who sin.

Note: There are several scenes of violence, and one inference of molestation.

{A Novel Treat}

… Galway's Black Bean Salsa

While stuck in the Sinner's house, Galway finds a can of black beans to satisfy his hunger. If he'd had some other ingredients, this is a recipe he could have made to satisfy his taste buds.

___one 15-ounce can black beans, drained and rinsed

___1½ cups frozen corn, thawed

___1 cup finely chopped sweet red pepper

___¾ cup finely chopped green pepper

___½ cup finely chopped red onion

___1 tablespoon minced fresh parsley

___½ cup sour cream

___¼ cup mayonnaise

___2 tablespoons red wine vinegar

___1 teaspoon ground cumin

___1 teaspoon chili powder

___½ teaspoon salt

___¼ teaspoon garlic powder

___⅛ teaspoon pepper

___tortilla chips

In a large bowl, combine the black beans, corn, peppers, onion, and parsley. In a separate bowl, combine the sour cream, mayonnaise, vinegar, and remaining seasonings. Pour sour cream mixture over the corn mixture and toss gently to coat. Makes enough dip for about 8 women.

Serve with tortilla chips and enjoy!

{Quotes from *Sinner*}

"How could God ever forgive a devil like me?" (Sinner)

"Because he is God. He does what he wants, whether you like it or not." (Maria Eliza)

{Pizazz}

A collection of journals is key to this story. Purchase a small, inexpensive journal and pen to present to each woman. Encourage your guests to record their own stories. Perhaps you'll even want to have a story-sharing session at a future gathering!

That's Interesting!

- There has been speculation about the identity of Ms. Rogers. Some think that she's really a popular secular author masquerading as a Christian writer, while others suppose Rogers is really a group of female Christian writers who collaboratively have written a mystery novel. Only she and her publisher know the truth.

- Rogers incorporates a number of references to comic book lore in her writing. See if you and your group and pick out any names or locations that relate to comic book heroes.

{Cracking the Spine}

Use these questions and comments to get women talking.

- What surprised you most in this story?

- What do you think gave Maria Eliza the courage to draw close to Sinner when everyone else pulled away?

- At one point Maria Eliza asks Galway, "Do you believe in miracles?" He replies, "Actually, my dear, I believe it takes more faith to disbelieve miracles than it does to believe them." What do you think about his statement?

- How are the experiences of the Sinner and Loftis Johnson similar? What is different between the two men?

- Sinner is unable to accept forgiveness and feels emotional torment. What is your own experience with accepting or rejecting forgiveness? Tell about a time when you experienced unexpected forgiveness.

- 1 Peter 4:12-13 says, "Dear friends, don't be surprised at the fiery trials you are going through, as if something strange were happening to you. Instead, be very glad—for these trials make you partners with Christ in his suffering, so that you will have the wonderful joy of seeing his glory when it is revealed to all the world." How did Sinner see God glorified through his life? How was God *not* glorified? Tell about a difficult circumstance from your own life and how you saw God glorified.

{The Reference Section}

You may want to use these additional Bible verses during your discussion.

- Psalm 103:12—God has removed our sins.

- 1 John 1:9—God will forgive our sins.

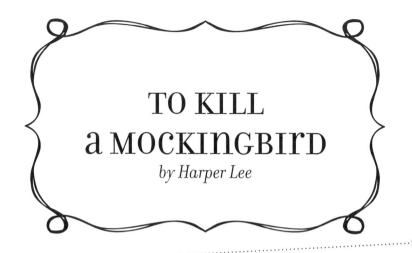

TO KILL a MOCKINGBIRD
by Harper Lee

{Book Review}

A Pulitzer Prize-winning novel in 1960, *To Kill a Mockingbird* uses a woman's childhood recollections to tell the story of life in a small Southern town. The narrative begins with Scout as a 6-year-old and ends about three years later, but the period in between is filled with her observations about an adult world that she finds complicated, perplexing, and sometimes unfair. With the help of their father, Atticus, she and her brother Jem struggle to understand people who are different from them. Hard lessons include a mysterious recluse, an elderly drug addict, a narrow-minded teacher, poverty-stricken families, town hypocrites, and even hurtful family members who actually mean well. Scout's world is really shaken in 1935, however, when Atticus agrees to defend a black man in court—against the desire of the townspeople.

Will justice be served?

{Critic's Comments}

To put it simply, this book is honest. It's about life. It's about us. True, it takes place in a specific American region during a specific era, but the

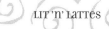

issues are real and the characters still matter to us—even after we've finished the last chapter.

{A Novel Treat}

... The Easiest Lane Cake in Maycomb County

Lane Cake originated in Alabama. Indeed, any good Southern cook can likely boast of a family recipe! None can beat this easy one, though—not even Aunt Alexandra's or Miss Maudie's.

Cake

___2 yellow or vanilla cake mixes and ingredients to make those as listed on package

Filling and Frosting

___8 egg yolks

___1¼ cups sugar

___⅓ cup grape or apple juice

___1 cup chopped pecans

___1 cup shredded coconut

___1 cup raisins

Following directions on the cake mix boxes, prepare batter and spread ¾ of it evenly among three 9-inch cake pans (you'll have batter left over—you can use this for cupcakes or another dessert). Bake cake layers according to directions. Cool for about 10 minutes, then remove cakes from pans and place on racks to cool completely.

For the filling, combine egg yolks and sugar in a heavy pan or double boiler. Cook over medium heat (don't boil), stirring constantly with a wooden spoon until mixture thickens. It should be of a consistency that will stick to the spoon. Remove mixture from heat, then add remaining ingredients.

When cake and filling are both thoroughly cooled, spread filling on top of two cakes, assemble the three layers, and frost entire cake with remaining mixture.

Serves 10.

{Quotes from *To Kill a Mockingbird*}

"You never really understand a person until you consider things from his point of view...until you climb into his skin and walk around in it." (Atticus Finch)

"I wanted you to see what real courage is, instead of getting the idea that courage is a man with a gun in his hand. It's when you know you're licked before you begin but you begin anyway and you see it through no matter what. You rarely win, but sometimes you do." (Atticus)

{Pizazz}

Boo Radley surprised Scout and Jem with small gifts in the hollow of a tree. Surprise your guests with an invitation fashioned after one of Boo's gifts: sticks of gum. Type or print invitation details on 2½x5-inch strips of paper (if you have a computer with a printer, copy multiple invitations on the same sheet, then cut into strips). Lay a foil-wrapped stick of double-mint gum at the end of each strip with the writing facing down, and then turn the stick over until the invitation covers the gum like an original wrapper would. Secure with tape.

That's Interesting!

To Kill a Mockingbird, voted in a Library Journal poll as "Best Novel of the Century," is considered an autobiographical account of Harper Lee's childhood. Like Scout, Harper was a tomboy and an avid reader, and her father was a lawyer in their small town in Alabama. Her childhood friend, Truman Capote, likely inspired the character of Dill.

{Cracking the Spine}

Use these questions and comments to get women talking.

- Discuss the significance of the novel's title. Who were the "mockingbirds" within the story? How so?

- Lee uses humor to diffuse—as in the school pageant scene. Why is humor so important to our often painful lives? What do you think is God's view of humor?

- While there's clear evidence of evil within this story, we also glimpse many simple acts of kindness (remember when "someone" covered Scout's shoulders with a blanket on the night of the fire?). Which show of kindness did you most appreciate? Why? Tell about a time when you were personally impacted by a simple act of kindness.

- Atticus Finch is one of America's most beloved literary characters. In your opinion, what are his strengths as a father? a lawyer? a friend? What are his weaknesses?

- Think of who you were when you were 8 years old. Do you think you'd have hung out with Scout and Jem? Why or why not? Considering her childhood, describe the woman you imagine Scout would become.

- The Bible tells us that if anyone has caused grief, we are to forgive and comfort that person (2 Corinthians 2:5-7). If you were Atticus or Helen Robinson or Jem, would you find it difficult to forgive Bob Ewell? Why or why not? How do we forgive those who seem unforgivable?

- This story has a sad ending. Honestly, it doesn't really seem like justice. How might God's idea of justice not always involve a "happy ending"? Give an example.

{The Reference Section}

You may want to use these additional Bible verses during your discussion.

- Matthew 23:27-28—The heart of a hypocrite.

- Colossians 3:12-14—Clothe yourself with love.

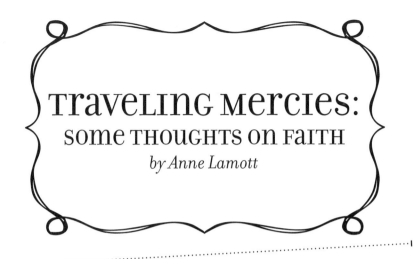

Traveling Mercies: Some Thoughts on Faith

by Anne Lamott

{Book Review}

While many have written about their faith journeys, this memoir is a boldly honest and witty encounter with one woman's unusual and often jagged walk of faith. Anne isn't exactly raised in a Christian home and is far from becoming a candidate for "Mother of the Year." She's had a fairly successful life as a novelist, but after the death of her father, her life spins out of control. She delves into deep depression, drug addiction and alcoholism, and a series of train-wreck relationships with men. Anne describes her Christian growth as it evolves from small sparks of hope during dark times of addiction and loneliness in her youth to moments of exuberant miracles that lead her to understand the strength and love she finds in God. Along the way, Anne discovers how to rely on the strength of friends and how to hold tightly on to God's unconditional love.

{Critic's Comments}

There's no question that this book will spark some lively discussion on what it means and looks like to be a Christian. Anne Lamott doesn't come across as a likeable person, and she certainly has not lived an angelic life. But women will laugh at the author's irreverence and might be shocked to discover some similarities in their lives and Anne's. Readers are likely to be moved by her moments of triumph, no matter how far out into left field she seems to be.

Note: This book does include the use of profanity and describes lifestyles and behaviors that can be deemed objectionable or inappropriate.

{A Novel Treat}

… Candle Salad

Anne learned how to make this traditional Jewish recipe when she was being indoctrinated by her college friends. At the base of the candle salad, add a note with this quote from the book: "Most of the people I know who have what I want…are people with a deep sense of spirituality…They follow a brighter light than the glimmer of their own candle; they are part of something beautiful."

____1 leaf of lettuce per person

____1 ring of pineapple per person

____half a banana per person

____1 orange slice per person

____1 maraschino cherry per person

____toothpicks

Place the lettuce leaf on a small plate and set on it a ring of pineapple. Add a banana half so it stands vertically in the middle of the ring. Place an orange slice on the side of the banana, and secure it to the pineapple with a toothpick. Add a maraschino cherry on top.

{Quotes from *Traveling Mercies*}

"Grace is the light or electricity or juice or breeze that takes you from that isolated place and puts you with others who are as startled and embarrassed and eventually grateful as you are to be there."

"Here are the two best prayers I know: 'Help me, help me, help me,' and 'Thank you, thank you, thank you.'"

{Pizazz}

Collect resealable baggies of dimes (one for each guest). You need only to add a few dimes per bag. Tie the bags with curling ribbon, and attach a note that reads, "Everyone needs a 'Mary Williams' in her life—let me be yours! Use this bag of dimes to be a 'Mary Williams' to someone else."

That's Interesting!

Anne also released a "sequel" memoir called *Plan B: Further Thoughts on Faith*. In it she continues the story of her faith walk as she approaches middle age; and her son—now a self-proclaimed right-wing Christian—approaches teenage years.

{Cracking the Spine}

Use these questions and comments to get women talking.

- Why do you think Anne, who seems almost annoyed with some parts of the service, continues to attend St. Andrew's church?

- Anne quotes a Leonard Cohen song that says, "There are cracks, cracks in everything, that's how the light gets in." Do you think "cracked" people are more likely to grow stronger spiritually than those who grow up in safe Christian homes? Explain your thoughts.

- Consider all the people who touch Anne's life, from those she is close to, to those with whom she has random encounters. Which do you think has most influenced Anne's growth as a Christian and why? Who are the people that have most influenced your growth as a Christian?

- What traveling mercies should you request?

- How does Anne rely on other authors for spiritual epiphanies? Why do you think she quotes more literary references than she does Scripture?

- Anne writes about her faith, "Mine was a patchwork God, sewn together from bits of rag and ribbon, Eastern and Western, pagan and Hebrew, everything but the kitchen sink and Jesus." Do you consider Anne's view of Christianity—even after her conversion—unorthodox? How is her worldview different from yours?

- Read about Paul's conversion in Acts 9:1-31. What similarities are there between Paul and Anne? How did the church and relationships play a part in their faith walks?

{The Reference Section }

You may want to use these additional Bible verses during your discussion.

- Romans 10:5-13—Salvation is for everyone.

- 2 Corinthians 5:3-7—We live by believing, and not by seeing.

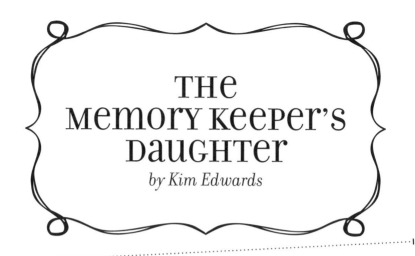

THE MEMORY KEEPER'S DAUGHTER

by Kim Edwards

{Book Review}

One stormy night during the winter of 1964, Dr. David Henry changes the course of not only his own life, but also the lives of his nurse, his wife, and their twin children. That night he begins a devastating secret when he sends his newborn daughter, Phoebe, to a home for the mentally infirm with nurse Caroline Gill and tells his wife that the baby has died. Caroline cannot bear to leave the child at the institution, and begins her own life of secrecy when she runs away with the baby, planning to raise Phoebe herself. Can David Henry fix this situation like he fixes broken bones? Or will his lies destroy the lives of those he only wants to protect?

{Critic's Comments}

This book deals with the theme of secret sins and the concentric circles of pain radiating out on others' lives. One act that seems small and even gracious at the start must be covered by more and more lies, and the consequences are devastating for some. The message is that ultimately it's never too late to make things right and begin the process of forgiveness.

Note: This book includes profanity, characters that abuse drugs and alcohol, and adultery.

{A Novel Treat}

... Raspberry Cake

Enjoy a slice of raspberry cake, as Paul did at the wedding. This recipe is easy and sure to please.

___1 white cake mix

___⅔ cup salad oil

___4 eggs

___one 4-ounce package raspberry gelatin

___one 10-ounce package frozen raspberries, thawed

___2 teaspoons raspberry flavoring

Mix all ingredients well. Bake either in layers or in a 9x13-inch cake pan. Bake at 350 degrees for 50 minutes. Top with whipped cream and garnish with fresh berries, if you like.

Serves 12.

{Quotes from *The Memory Keeper's Daughter*}

"Her secrets, like his own, had grown up into a wall between them."

"You're defending him," he said slowly.

"No. I'm forgiving him. I'm trying to, anyway. There's a difference." (Paul and Norah)

{Pizazz}

Photography plays a key role in David Henry's life. Use this element from the story on your invitation.

Create and send an invitation with a black-and-white photograph of a solitary tree, a vase of daffodils, or the beach. You might even ask your guests to bring photographs that they think reflect the style of art David chose.

That's Interesting!

Kim Edwards started teaching college English and decided to get a second Master's degree in teaching English as a second language.

After receiving her second master's degree and marrying, she and her husband lived in remote locations in Malaysia, Japan, and Cambodia where she totally immersed herself in the language and culture. These experiences led her to write a variety of short stories.

{Cracking the Spine}

Use these questions and comments to get women talking.

- As Dr. David Henry drives his wife to the clinic he stops at every stop sign even though his wife is in intense pain. What does this tell you about Dr. Henry? How does knowing this information about Dr. Henry help you in understanding the decision he made just hours later?

- This story clearly demonstrates that one lie needs another. How have you seen this truth played out around you in your own life or the lives of others you know?

- Throughout the novel, people reacted differently to Phoebe and the others with Downs syndrome. How did you feel when Dr. Henry sent his daughter to a facility for the mentally impaired? How has society's view of children with Downs syndrome changed over the past 40 years? As Christians, how should we view people with a disability?

- What ways did each of the main characters deal with their pain? How might their situations have been different if they had turned to God for help in dealing with loss? How are you most likely to deal with pain or loss?

- David says, "Photography is all about secrets. The secrets we all have and will never tell." Do you think we all have secrets we never tell? Compare David's comment to the truth of Psalm 90:8, which says, "You spread out our sins before you—our secret sins—and you see them all." How do you feel about the fact that God is all-knowing and that we cannot hide secrets from him?

{The Reference Section}

You may want to use these additional Bible verses during your discussion.

- Luke 17:4—Repeated forgiveness.

- Psalm 139:1—God knows everything about us.

A Thread of Grace
by Mary Doria Russell

{Book Review}

Late in World War II, thousands of Jewish refugees escape into the Italian countryside, hoping to find safety. But when alliances change they are no longer safe and must depend on the kindness of the poor Italian villagers for survival. Families are split, chaos is everywhere, and everyone is desperate to stay alive. Mixed in are the intersecting stories of spies, Resistance fighters, a repentant German defector, a rabbi, and a Catholic priest.

A Thread of Grace is a complex and haunting story with vibrant characters that endear themselves to your heart. Mary Doria Russell takes the facts and personalizes them with heart-wrenching accounts that will make the reader weep with both sadness and joy.

{Critic's Comments}

The number of characters makes this book seem daunting at first, but once you meet them all, the story moves quickly and becomes engrossingly compelling. The accounts told here make you believe in the goodness of mankind even in the most horrible circumstances. Honestly, the heroes and heroines leave you breathless.

Note: This story takes place during a war, so there is wartime violence but nothing is overly graphic. A rape is implied but not described.

{A Novel Treat}

... Mirella's Mandlebrodt

Jewish Mandlebrodt (or Mandelbread) means "almond bread," a twice-baked cake very similar to Italian biscotti. Serve this dessert with coffee or tea in honor of the Jewish-Italian heroes of the story's alpine region.

____1 egg

____½ cup sugar

____3 tablespoons oil

____1½ cups flour

____1½ cups blanched almonds, chopped

Whisk the egg, sugar, and flour together. When the mixture is thick, fold in flour and salt. Add almonds. Place dough in a greased loaf pan, then bake at 350 degrees for about 30 minutes.

Invert bread onto wire rack, cool, then slice through with a serrated knife at ½-inch intervals. Place these slices on a cookie sheet, return to oven, and bake for 10 minutes. Flip slices over and bake for an additional 6 minutes or until golden. Cool completely and store up to one week in an airtight container.

Note: Slices will be crisp—these are best when dunked in coffee or tea.

Makes about 12 pieces.

{Quotes from *A Thread of Grace*}

"What you feel is not contrition, my son. It's dread. I can't absolve a fear of hell." (Don Osvaldo Tomitz)

"No matter how dark the tapestry God weaves for us, there's always a thread of grace." (Iacopo Soncini, repeating a Hebrew saying)

{Pizazz}

Find gold-colored braid or string in the notions section of your local fabric store, and purchase enough to cut one 10-inch length for each of your guests. After your book group has discussed *A Thread of Grace*, present each guest with a length of string as a reminder of the grace we receive from God. Suggest that they tie these "threads of grace" where they'll see them often as meaningful mementos or use them as bookmarks in the next book your group reads.

That's Interesting!

It took Mary Doria Russell seven years to write this book, but much of that time was spent on her extensive research. And, determined to strike an emotional cord with her readers so they'd be able to connect with the historical aspect of the story, she painstakingly developed each major character and event. Such diligence paid off: *A Thread of Grace* was nominated for a Pulitzer Prize.

{Cracking the Spine}

Use these questions and comments to get women talking.

- This was a story of sacrifice. Which character's sacrifice most resonated with you? Why? Most of us can't imagine life in a war-torn country, but we still witness day-to-day sacrifices in our own lives—even if they're on a much smaller scale. Tell us about a sacrifice that someone has made for you.

- Mirella tells Iacopa that he's done enough—that as a man with his own family, he should hide rather than risk capture by helping to save others. How do you feel about her demands? How do we balance our personal lives with "the bigger cause"?

- During a conversation with Schramm, Mirella makes the ironic statement that it's "distressing to be hated because of lies…" Have you ever been misjudged or have you misjudged others? What happened?

- In Matthew 5:39 Jesus says: "Do not resist an evil person! If someone slaps you on the right cheek, offer the other also." How do we reconcile this with the words of the Red Priest who said, "If you refuse to oppose those who do harm, you are complicit"?

- When Simon asked Maria about her political views, or which side she was on, she described the conflicting politics of the Germans, Fascists, Communists, and the Black Brigades and replied that "broken clocks are correct two times a day." What do you think she meant by that? Do you agree or disagree? How could that relate to today's politics?

- It's ironic that Italy, a fascist country occupied by Nazis, had the highest number of Jewish survivors during World War II. What other events or facts within the story did you find ironic? For example, think of those involving:

  Renzo Leoni and his aliases

  Don Osvaldo Tomitz and Werner Schramm

  Maria Avoni's role in the fighting effort

  Werner Schramm and Mirella Soncini

- When she left Europe after the war, Claudia hid significant pieces of her history—even from her own children. Why do you think she did that? Would you have done the same thing? Why or why not? What can her experience teach us about making assumptions about people we don't know?

- The very last line of the book consists of this "one last awful thought: all the harm he ever did was done for him by others." What is your reaction to this?

{The Reference Section }

You may want to use these additional Bible verses during your discussion.

- Exodus 34:5-7—The blessings and consequences that travel through generations.

- John 15:13—The greatest love of all.

THE LAST SIN EATER
by Francine Rivers

{Book Review}

Set in the Great Smoky Mountains during the mid-1850s, *The Last Sin Eater* tells the story of 10-year-old Cadi, a girl who is gripped by the guilt of sin. Her only hope of forgiveness is through the "sin eater," a man who is given food to take on the sins of the deceased, but must be shunned by all the others because of his role. Not wanting to live with the guilt of her sin, Cadi searches the mountains to find the sin eater, hoping to convince him to enact the ritual while she lives. At the same time an evangelist enters the valley, and finds his life threatened by the men who live there. Will Cadi find the hope she's looking for, or will the darkness of sin continue to enslave the valley?

{Critic's Comments}

This is a book full of passion, secrets, and pursuit. It's a love story of forgiveness between mothers and daughters, friends, a community, and a young girl and Christ. Women will identify not only with Cadi's questions and fears, but her longing for love, as well.

This is a compelling and touching story that's also filled with the gospel message.

... Cadi's Chocolate Angel Food Cake

This is a cake that Cadi's own angel, Lilybet, would love.

Cake

___1½ cups egg whites (about 10)

___1 cup cake flour

___2 cups sugar, divided

___½ cup baking cocoa

___1 teaspoon cream of tartar

___1 teaspoon vanilla extract

___¼ teaspoon salt

Glaze

___½ cup semisweet chocolate chips

___3 tablespoons half-and-half cream

Place egg whites in a large mixing bowl and let them stand at room temperature for about 30 minutes.

In another bowl, sift together the flour, 1 cup of sugar, and the cocoa twice. Set aside.

Add the cream of tartar, vanilla, and salt to the egg whites, and beat on medium speed until soft peaks form. Gradually beat in the remaining sugar on high until stiff, glossy peaks form and the sugar is dissolved. Slowly fold in the flour mixture, about a ½ cup at a time. Gently spoon into an ungreased 10-inch tube pan, and cut through the batter with a knife to remove any air pockets.

Bake on the lowest oven rack at 350 degrees for 40-50 minutes or until lightly browned and the entire top appears dry. Immediately invert the pan and cool completely. Run a knife around the sides and center of the pan to release the cake, and place the cake on a serving plate.

For the glaze, place chocolate chips and cream in a microwave-safe bowl, heating for 1-minute intervals until chocolate is melted. Stir until smooth and then drizzle over the cake.

Serves 8.

{Quotes from *The Last Sin Eater*}

"Death is all around me. It's right here with me." (Cadi)

"So is life. You must choose." (Lilybet)

{Pizazz}

Use the gift of honey as a gift for your guests. Find small decorative jars and fill them with honey. Put a label on the outside that says, "Bletsung's Best Honey," and give to each woman as she leaves.

That's Interesting!

In *The Last Sin Eater* the salvation of many adults is accomplished through one small girl. Francine Rivers' own salvation was brought about by an 8-year-old neighbor boy who invited her to church.

The idea of sin eating has roots in several cultures. The 1911 *Encyclopaedia Britannica* states, "...in the Balkan peninsula a small bread image of the deceased is made and eaten by the survivors of the family. The Dutch *doed-koecks* or 'dead-cakes,' marked with the initials of the deceased, introduced into America in the 17th century, were long given to the attendants at funerals in old New York. The 'burial-cakes' which are still made in parts of rural England, for example Lincolnshire and Cumberland, are almost certainly a relic of sin-eating."

{Cracking the Spine}

Use these questions and comments to get women talking.

- Why did Miz Elda encourage Cadi and Fagan to seek the sin eater when everyone else discouraged this?

- Discuss the key relationships in the book, and how they changed through the course of the story. Consider Cadi and her mother, Miz Elda and Iona, and Fagan and Cadi.

- In what ways did the Kai hold the valley captive? How does our sin hold us captive?

- Cadi is drawn to Christ out of her deep need for forgiveness, while Fagan yearns for Christ's love. Briefly describe what circumstances or people drew you to Christ.

- At the end of the book, Sim says, "…all I was ever able to do was eat the bread and drink the wine. It was nothing but an empty ceremony. It accomplished nothing." What do you find yourself tempted to place your hope in, instead of Christ?

- 1 Peter 3:15 says, "Instead, you must worship Christ as Lord of your life. And if someone asks about your Christian hope, always be ready to explain it." What threatened to keep Cadi from telling others about the hope she found? What keeps you from telling others?

{The Reference Section}

You may want to use these additional Bible verses during your discussion.

- Isaiah 61:1-3—Good news for the brokenhearted.

- John 3:17—Salvation through Jesus Christ.

AT Home
In MITForD
by Jan Karon

{Book Review}

Father Tim feels not only worn-out in his small town parish; he fears he might even be useless. Then his quiet parish life makes a sudden turn when a dog (the size of a Buick) barrels into his life; an 11-year-old boy uses his bathroom; disease rages through his body; a new cleaning woman takes over his home; and a beautiful woman moves in next door, blazing a path through his hedge and his heart. Throw in a beautiful mountain village peopled with colorful characters reminiscent of small towns everywhere and you will feel right at home as you wonder: Will Father Tim adjust to the massive changes in his life or die trying?

{Critic's Comments}

This book deals with the themes of rest and restoration with a liberal dash of romance and a strong dose of good old-fashioned common sense. It's sure to warm women's hearts!

Note: While for the most part this book is wholesome and encouraging, one character is shot.

{A Novel Treat}

… Poached Pears and Chocolate Sauce

While entertaining his beautiful neighbor, Father Tim served poached pears and coffee on a silver tray. This quick-to-fix recipe will sweeten your time together also.

Pears

____⅓ cup sugar

____¼ cup orange juice

____¾ cup water

____2½ to 3 inches of stick cinnamon

____1 teaspoon vanilla

____4 medium pears, peeled, halved, and cored

In skillet, bring sugar, orange juice, cinnamon stick, vanilla, and water to boil. Add pears and then reduce heat. Simmer, covered, for 10-15 minutes or until pears are tender. Remove cinnamon sticks. Serve drained and chilled with vanilla ice cream and hot Fudge Sauce. Serves 4.

Fudge Sauce

____½ cup butter

____½ cup cocoa

____½ teaspoon salt

____¼ cup white corn syrup

____3 cups sugar

____1 can evaporated milk

____1 teaspoon vanilla

Combine butter, cocoa, salt, and syrup. Heat over low heat. Gradually add sugar. Stir slowly and thoroughly. It will be thick. When mixed, add evaporated milk. Heat until sugar is dissolved and mixture is thick and creamy. Add vanilla. Store in refrigerator. Holds well and doesn't get sugary.

{Quotes from *At Home in Mitford*}

"In the space of precisely seven minutes, which he reckoned to be the full length of her visit, he had been told a terrible truth, discovered an answer to prayer, helped someone find a ministry, and been unutterably refreshed in his own spirit. Perhaps, he thought, we should all live as if we're dying."

"One of the things that makes a dead leaf fall to the ground is the bud of the new leaf that pushes it off the limb. When you let God fill you with his love and forgiveness, the things you think you desperately want to hold on to start falling away...and we hardly notice their passing."

{Pizazz}

Set your table with a lovely tablecloth and break out the family china as Father Tim did for Cynthia while dining on poached pears and chocolate sauce. Gather any other items that make you feel "at home" and use them to help your guests feel comfortable. Or ask everyone to bring her favorite item that makes her feel "at home" and use those as a conversation starter.

That's Interesting!

The coma-inducing orange marmalade cake raved about from chapter to chapter did not exist until Jan Karon wrote *At Home in Mitford*. From the first mention of the famed cake, readers requested the recipe…but no recipe was to be had. When Karon was hired by Victoria magazine to be their writer-in-residence, editor Claire Whitcomb decided a recipe should be created. Scott Peacock and Ms. Edna Lewis, both legendary chefs, put their heads together and came up with a recipe for the now infamous orange marmalade cake.

{Cracking the Spine}

Use these questions and comments to get women talking.

- If you could get away for a time of rest and renewal as Father Tim did, where would you go and why?

- Absalom Greer said, "Resting. Sometimes we get so worn out with being useful that we get useless. I'll ask you what another preacher once asked: Are you too exhausted to run and too scared to rest?" How would you answer that question?

- Father Tim asks Cynthia, "Would you agree that we must be willing to thank God for every trial of our faith, no matter how severe, for the greater strength it produces?" What do you think? What are the trials that have grown you the most in your life?

- Throughout the story, Father Tim experiences a general feeling of unrest; something wasn't right, but he couldn't put his finger on it. Have you experienced such a time? Were the consequences as serious as Father Tim's or did you read the signs sooner?

- When was the last time you were astounded by the weight of sorrow in the world? What did you do about it, if anything?

- Miss Sadie spoke of her mother's favorite Bible verse. Do you have a favorite verse? One you have modeled your life after? If so, share it. In fact, you might all want to write down the references of each other's favorite verses to keep as inspiration and encouragement.

- Miss Sadie felt an enormous weight shift when her secrets were shared with another. Have you had a similar experience you're willing to share? Why would a burden be lifted when a secret is exposed?

{The Reference Section }

You may want to use these additional Bible verses during your discussion.

- Philippians 4:13—We can do anything with Christ's strength.

- Matthew 6:10—Prayer for God's will to be done.

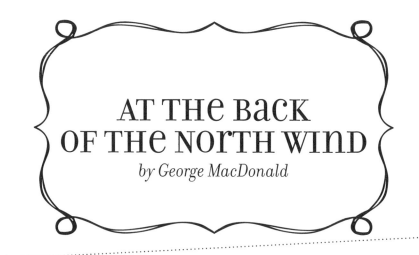

At the Back of the North Wind
by George MacDonald

{Book Review}

In this classic tale, Diamond, a young boy who befriends a spirit-lady called the North Wind, travels with her in a place between asleep and awake. The lessons he learns from her and the strength of his own character help shelter him from upcoming sorrows and hardships of life.

This simple story with its simplistic tone reminds us of a time when we too had the ability to believe without questions and love without reason.

{Critic's Comments}

Women will enjoy this nostalgic trip through childhood fantasies. In the midst of "real world" decisions and realities women face day to day, this story is a refreshing escape to naïve innocence and childlike faith. Although considered children's literature, the book explores social injustice, the role of death in our lives, and a deep need for both love and forgiveness.

{A Novel Treat}

... Tea and Crumpets

Purchase a box of Earl Gray tea (or another favorite tea), prepare, and serve with these crumpets for a snack like Diamond and his family enjoyed.

___1 cup warm water

___1 cup warm milk

___2 tablespoons melted butter

___½ teaspoon baking soda dissolved in ¼ cup warm water

___3½ cups flour

___2 teaspoons sugar

___2 teaspoons salt

___2½ teaspoons dry yeast

___additional butter for cooking

In a large bowl, dissolve yeast in water and let stand for 5 minutes. Add sugar, salt, butter, and milk. Gradually add flour until the batter has a slight elastic consistency. Cover and let stand for 45 minutes. Add the dissolved baking soda, re-cover, and allow 20-30 minutes for the batter to rise.

Grease griddle with butter and drop ¼ cup of batter, spacing 2 inches apart. Reduce heat to low and cover griddle. Crumpets will cook about 15 minutes, or until the crumpets' tops look dry. Do not turn over! The crumpets may look gummy, but will be done.

Toast the crumpets before serving and try topping with butter and honey. Makes 15 servings.

{Quotes from *At the Back of the North Wind*}

"Only he knew that to be left alone is not always to be forsaken."

"But to try to make others comfortable is the only way to get right comfortable ourselves, and that comes partly of not being able to think so much about ourselves when we are helping other people. For our Selves will always do pretty well if we don't pay them too much attention."

"The whole ways and look of the child, so full of quiet wisdom, yet so ready to accept the judgment of others in his own dispraise, took hold of my heart, and I felt myself wonderfully drawn towards him."

{Pizazz}

Return to the days of reciting nursery rhymes and rewrite your favorite rhyme to incorporate the important information, including the book title, author, time, and place. With double stick tape, adhere your new poem to a piece of patterned scrapbooking paper for an invitation that sets the tone for your guests' arrival.

That's Interesting!

According to some in author George MacDonald's family, the character Diamond may be loosely based upon Maurice, one of MacDonald's sons, who died at a young age.

{Cracking the Spine}

Use these questions and comments to get women talking.

- Like most fantasies, this story is filled with metaphors. Which one struck you as most meaningful?

- Why do you think the author consistently reminds us throughout the story that Diamond had been to the back of the north wind?

- How was the author's use of nursery rhymes similar to or different from Jesus' use of parables? Consider the rhyme about Little Bo Peep in chapter 28.

- What was the relevance of Nanny's dream when she was on the brink of death? How was it different from Diamond's when he was ill? Do you think dreams seem more vivid or intense when the dreamer is ill?

- In Romans 8:28, Paul says, "And we know that God causes everything to work together for the good of those who love God and are called according to his purpose for them." How does this compare with the North Wind's explanation to Diamond: "I could not be cruel if I would. I can do nothing cruel, although I often do what looks like cruel to those who do not know what I really am doing"? Why do we instinctively seem to blame God when bad things happen?

- Diamond said that on the back of the North Wind, a person could sit among the branches of a tree and watch, unnoticed, as family and friends carry on with their lives. If given the chance, would you want the ability to watch your loved ones without them knowing? Do you think such a thing will be possible in heaven?

- The North Wind exposes her identity to Diamond in chapter 36. Share your thoughts about the revelation.

{The Reference Section}

You may want to use these additional Bible verses during your discussion.

- 1 Corinthians 13:1-13—Definition of love.

- Mark 10:14-15—Jesus welcomes children.

Gaudy Night

by Dorothy L. Sayers

{Book Review}

Harriet D. Vane, mystery writer and amateur detective, finds trouble in a cloak sleeve when she attends a Gaudy night at her alma mater, Shrewsbury Women's College in Oxford, England. As she works to untangle the threads of clues left hither and yon at Shrewsbury she also works to solve the mystery of her heart. Calling in Lord Peter Wimsey to help with the case intensifies the activities of the poltergeist as well as the feelings twining round in Miss Vane's heart and mind. Will Harriet choose the intellectual life over one of marital bliss or will the "Poltergeist" of Shrewsbury take the decision out of her hands forever?

{Critic's Comments}

Written in the 1930s, this book deals with the still present and often controversial theme of a woman's place in this world. Put this together with a thrilling mystery and a handsome detective and readers will find it difficult to put down until the last page has been read!

Note: Book contains mild language, suggestion of murder, and talk of sexual affairs.

{A Novel Treat}

... Meringue Shells

Like Miss Vane, make up a batch of meringues for the entertainment of your friends.

___3 egg whites

___1 teaspoon vanilla

___¼ teaspoon cream of tartar

___1 cup sugar

___dash of salt

Let egg whites stand in large mixing bowl until room temperature (about 1 hour). Cover your cookie sheet with brown paper, drawing eight 3-inch circles on paper.

Add vanilla, cream of tartar, and salt to egg whites and beat with an electric mixer on medium speed until peaks form. Slowly add sugar, beating on high speed until peaks stand straight up and sugar is dissolved.

Drop meringue by tablespoon onto the brown paper spreading it throughout the circle building the sides up. You can also put the meringue through a pastry tube (or plastic bag with a corner clipped off) tracing the inner edge of penciled circle if you like.

Bake at 300 degrees for 35 minutes. Turn off oven and let shells dry in the oven for an hour.

Fill with pudding or fruit and whipped cream.

Makes eight shells.

{Quotes from *Gaudy Night*}

"She went to bed thinking more about another person than about herself. This goes to prove that even minor poetry may have its practical uses."

"I admit it is better fun to punt than to be punted, and that a desire to have all the fun is nine-tenths of the law of chivalry." (Lord Peter Wimsey)

"Is it possible that you have a just and generous mind? I will not be outdone in generosity. I will sit like a perfect lady and watch you do the work. It's nice to see things done well." (Harriet Vane)

{Pizazz}

According to the *American Heritage Dictionary*, a *gaudy night* is "a feast, especially an annual university dinner." On these occasions, guests dressed to the "nines" so to speak, pulling out their best finery. Create an invitation to a "Gaudy Night" book club, inviting the women in your group to dress in their best finery (or perhaps in silly finery—that's up to you!). Remind them to wear their thinking caps for an evening of deep discussion!

That's Interesting!

The daughter of a minister, Dorothy L. Sayers claimed that religion and medieval studies were subjects more worthy of her time than writing detective stories. She spent the last years of her life working on an English translation of *Dante's Divine Comedy*. She also wrote many plays, essays, and radio broadcasts on Christian themes.

{Cracking the Spine}

Use these questions and comments to get women talking.

- Many characters are put forth as the guilty party. Whom did you believe to be guilty? When did you realize who was the real criminal?

- Early on, Harriet reveals herself to have an inferiority complex that affects how she feels about Lord Peter Wimsey. How does her view of herself change throughout the story? When have people or events caused you to change your view of yourself?

- Harriet says, "A woman may achieve greatness, or at any rate great renown, by merely being a wonderful wife and mother… whereas the men who have achieved great renown by being devoted husbands and fathers might be counted on the fingers of one hand." Share your thoughts and experiences as they relate to this quote.

- Miss de Vine states, "However painful it is, there's always one thing one has to deal with sincerely, if there's any root to one's mind at all." What is your "one thing"?

- This book includes discussion on women being a part of the work force. Written in the 1930s, this idea was certainly not the norm. Share your thoughts on the roles of women today. Would you agree with Harriet or with Beatrice's mother?

- Why do you believe Harriet Vane chose to accept Lord Peter Wimsey's proposal at the end of the book? How did the mystery change Harriet's view of marriage? Or of Lord Peter Wimsey?

{The Reference Section}

You may want to use these additional Bible verses during your discussion.

- Matthew 10:34—Peace or a sword?

- Matthew 26:75—Peter's denial of Christ.

GIFT from THE Sea

by Anne Morrow Lindbergh

{Book Review}

Initially famous for being the wife of aviator Charles Lindbergh, Anne Morrow Lindbergh later became known for her reflective writing. In *Gift from the Sea* she writes, "I have learned…that certain rules of conduct are more conducive to inner and outer harmony than others. There are, in fact, certain roads that one may follow. Simplification of life is one of them."

Anne's practical dealing with the topics of simplicity, patience, contentedness, purpose, relationship and the co-mingling of each in the complexity of life with spouse, family, work, and church ring just as true today as when she wrote of them years ago. Journey with Anne as she plumbs the depths of her heart in her time of solitude, and sample the gifts from the sea she finds on the way.

{Critic's Comments}

Even though this book was published in 1955, Lindbergh addresses timeless issues that are current even today. Women will readily relate to the struggles she shares, and those who are reflective in nature will especially appreciate her wholesome insights.

{A Novel Treat}

... Cinnamon-Apple Corn Bread

Enjoy a slice of deliciously moist, noncrumbly cornbread and a cup of coffee as Anne and her husband did on a rare quiet morning.

___1¼ cups yellow cornmeal

___¾ cup all-purpose flour

___⅓ cup sugar

___1 tablespoon baking powder

___½ teaspoon salt

___½ teaspoon cinnamon

___1 egg

___¾ cup sweet applesauce

___¼ cup oil

Stir together the cornmeal, flour, sugar, baking powder, salt, and cinnamon. Blend the egg, applesauce, and oil together and add to the dry ingredients. Blend just until moistened.

Pour into a greased 8-inch baking pan and bake at 350 degrees for 20-25 minutes. Serves 9.

{Quotes from *A Gift from the Sea*}

"Purposeful giving is not as apt to deplete one's resources; it belongs to that natural order of giving that seems to renew itself even in the act of depletion."

"A simple enough pleasure, surely, to have breakfast alone with one's husband, but how seldom married people in the midst of life achieve it."

{Pizazz}

Bring the ocean into your home. Decorate tables and shelves with shells, carefully placed handfuls of clean sand, and other items that remind you of the beach. Candles can be nestled into mounds of sand or tucked into larger shells. You can also play a CD of ocean sounds to further enhance your atmosphere.

At the end of your evening, give each woman one of the shells you used in your decorations, sharing these words from Anne as you present the gifts:

"That woman must be still as the axis of a wheel in the midst of her activities; that she must be the pioneer in achieving this stillness, not only for her own salvation, but for the salvation of family life, of society, perhaps even of our civilization."

That's Interesting!

Anne Morrow Lindbergh flew solo for the first time in 1929 and, in 1930, became the first American woman to earn a first class glider pilot's license. In 1934, the National Geographic Society awarded her the Hubbard Medal for having completed 40,000 miles of exploratory flying with Charles.

{Cracking the Spine}

Use these questions and comments to get women talking.

- If you could get away, either alone or with your husband or a special friend, where would you go?

- Simplification seems to be easier said than done. Anne talks first of the simplification of the outward life: clothes, shelter, activities. She then goes on to say this is not enough, but it is a start toward simplification of the inward life as well. Have you found ways to simplify your outward life? Has simplifying your outward life helped to simplify your inward life? If so, how?

- While discussing the role of the church in a woman's search to find space and solitude, Lindbergh asks the question, "But are those who attend as ready to give themselves or to receive its message as they used to be?" How would you respond to that question—for women in general and for yourself specifically?

- Anne suggests women will be more prepared for life in the home, in the community, and in the church if they spend: "Quiet time alone, contemplation, prayer, music, a centering line of thought or reading, of study or work." Compare this to our spiritual need for quiet time with God. What truths does Anne share that relate to you spiritually?

- When writing on middle age, Anne asserts, "Perhaps one can shed at this stage in life as one sheds in beach-living; one's pride, one's false ambitions, one's mask, one's armor.... Perhaps one can at last in middle age, if not earlier, be completely oneself. And what a liberation that would be!" If you are at or past "middle" age (you can define that yourself!), have you found this comment to be true? Or how have you seen it demonstrated in the lives of others who are ahead of you in life?

• Out of the many shells Anne found, she chose only a few to represent her time away. She notes that we usually select the known and seldom the strange. When was the last time you chose the unknown or strange? What happened?

{The Reference Section }

You may want to use these additional Bible verses during your discussion.

• Psalm 98:4—Sing for joy!

• Matthew 16:25—Give your life to Jesus.

THE HISTORY OF LOVE

by Nicole Krauss

{Book Review}

Leo Gursky, a Jewish immigrant who fled Poland to escape the horrors of World War II, is 78 years old, alone, and tormented by the insignificance of his life. Alma Singer is 14 years old and longs for her mother, Charlotte, to find happiness after the death of Alma's father. When Charlotte, a gifted linguist, receives a request to translate a book called *The History of Love*, Alma embarks on a quest to bring her mother happiness, triggering a series of events that weave the lives of Leo and Alma together in completely unexpected ways.

The story is told primarily by Leo and Alma, and readers must pay careful attention to piece together the puzzle of their increasingly connected lives.

{Critic's Comments}

The book explores classic themes of love, loss, forgiveness, and hope with astonishing poignancy and humor. There are no villains in this tale— only flawed human beings with universal wants and needs. Leo Gursky's character, especially, will touch the heart of every reader and remain there long after the last page is turned.

Note: This book does use objectionable language.

{A Novel Treat}

... Bruno's Cake

In one of the book's most memorable scenes, Leo comes home to find a mess in his kitchen and, in the middle of it all, a cake with yellow icing and the message, "Look who baked a cake." Here's a recipe for a lemon cake that is sure to please your guests as much as Bruno's cake pleased Leo—without the mess!

Cake

____1⅓ cups sugar

____6 tablespoons butter, softened

____1 tablespoon grated lemon rind

____3 tablespoons thawed lemonade concentrate

____2 teaspoons vanilla

____2 large eggs

____2 large egg whites

____2 cups flour

____1 teaspoon baking powder

____½ teaspoon salt

____½ teaspoon baking soda

____1¼ cups fat-free buttermilk

Preheat oven to 350 degrees.

Coat two 9-inch baking pans with cooking spray.

In a large bowl, mix sugar, butter, lemon rind, lemonade concentrate, and vanilla. Blend at medium speed until well blended. One at a time, add eggs and egg whites, beating well after each.

In a separate bowl, combine flour, baking powder, salt, and baking soda. Whisk until thoroughly blended. Alternately add flour mixture and buttermilk to sugar mixture, beginning and ending with flour mixture. Beat well after each addition.

Pour batter into baking pans. Bake at 350 degrees for 20 minutes or until a toothpick inserted in the center comes out clean. Cool in pans for 10 minutes; invert onto wire racks to cool.

Frosting

___2 tablespoons butter, room temperature

___2 teaspoons grated lemon rind

___2 teaspoons thawed lemonade concentrate

___½ teaspoon vanilla

___8 ounces ⅓-less-fat cream cheese, chilled

___1 drop yellow food coloring

___3½ cups powdered sugar

___pink decorating icing or gel

In a mixing bowl, beat butter, lemon rind, lemonade concentrate, vanilla, and cream cheese at high speed until fluffy. Add food coloring. Add powdered sugar and beat at low speed just until blended. (Be sure not to over beat.) Chill 1 hour.

Place one cake layer, topside down, on serving plate. Frost top. Place second layer, bottom-side down, on first layer. Frost sides, then top. Using pink decorating icing or gel, write on top of the cake, "Look who baked a cake!"

Cover loosely, and store in refrigerator. (This cake is good chilled or at room temperature.)

Makes 12 servings.

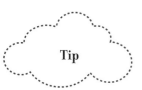

Tip

Just for fun, scatter your mixing bowl, spatula, eggshells, and measuring spoons and cups around your serving area. Before your guests arrive, set out the cake, and sprinkle flour around the cake and utensils. Your guests' faces will light up as they immediately recognize the scene from the book!

{Quotes from *The History of Love*}

"I'm a man who wanted to be as large as life." (Leo Gursky)

"Maybe this is how I'll go, in a fit of laughter, what could be better, laughing and crying, laughing and singing, laughing so as to forget that I am alone, that it is the end of my life, that death is waiting outside the door for me." (Leo Gursky)

{Pizazz}

On several sheets of parchment paper, write, in longhand, an excerpt from Leo's manuscript, *The History of Love*. Then quickly dip the pages in water (or, better yet, tea) and allow them to dry. Cut the sheets into invitation-sized rectangles. Then type and print out an invitation that you can paste over the parchment, leaving enough of the parchment visible to act as a border.

If this is too time-consuming, tear out several pages of a book you know you'll never read and use the pages as a background for your invitation.

That's Interesting!

Nicole Krauss was only 28 years old when her first book, *Man Walks into a Room,* was published, and she was 30 years old when *The History of Love* was published. She is married to novelist Jonathan Safran Foer (*Everything Is Illuminated, Extremely Loud, and Incredibly Close*). The couple doesn't read each other's books until they're about to be published!

{Cracking the Spine}

Use these questions and comments to get women talking.

- In spite of all the pain of his past, his present loneliness, and the imminence of his death, Leo wrote, "A wave of happiness came over me. It felt giddy to be part of it all." What do you think enabled Leo to experience this kind of joy?

- Leo worried that he would die on a day that he went unseen, so he made a point of being seen even if it made him appear ridiculous. What do you think prompted his need to be in some way significant? Do you feel this need is universal? What are some other ways that it is manifested?

- What role did Bruno play in Leo's life? Has there ever been a time in your life when you, like Leo, could say, "The truth is the thing I invented so I could live"?

- Leo's life embodied the truth of Romans 5:3-4: "We can rejoice, too, when we run into problems and trials, for we know that they help us develop endurance. And endurance develops strength of character, and character strengthens our confident hope of salvation." Discuss the role suffering has played in your life or the life of someone you know.

- Why do you think Zvi's wife, Rosa, refused to listen when he tried to confess his secret to her? What are some ways we, as wives, sometimes force our husbands into dishonesty?

- If you were to write your own obituary, what three adjectives or nouns would you use to describe yourself?

- This book explores many themes: life, death, love, loss, hope, and forgiveness. For you, what's the heart of this book's message?

{The Reference Section}

You may want to use these additional Bible verses during your discussion.

- Proverbs 13:12—Hope deferred or a dream fulfilled.

- Lamentations 3:31-32—God's compassion.

REDEMPTION

by Gary Smalley and Karen Kingsbury

{Book Review}

Professor Tim Jacobs' decision to leave his wife, Kari, for his gifted journalism student, Angela Manning, turns Kari's world upside down. Kari's family supports her as best they know how, but her decision to save her marriage at all costs stuns some members of her family. Struggling with her husband, her family, morning sickness, and God, Kari's defenses are low when she runs into her old flame. Misunderstandings from the past and confusion about her future force Kari to really look at her life. Will she and Tim be able to work through his unfaithfulness? Will Kari continue to rely on God throughout the whole ordeal? Will she remain faithful even if her husband has not?

{Critic's Comments}

This book deals with the themes of unfaithfulness and redemption in an honest, emotion-packed setting. Women are sure to see someone they know in this account of a marriage gone wrong, and the question of how far to extend forgiveness after an affair is one that is sure to spark discussion.

… Apple Pie and Ice Cream

Just as the Baxters enjoyed a time of conversation and fellowship over a slice of pie and ice cream, you'll enjoy this all-American dessert.

pie filling

___6 cups apples, peeled, cored, and thinly sliced

___¾ cup sugar

___1 tablespoon cinnamon

___1 tablespoon flour

Mix together apples, sugar, cinnamon, and flour. Set aside while you prepare pie crust.

Pastry for double-crust pie

___2 cups all-purpose flour

___½ teaspoon salt

___⅔ cup shortening

___6-7 tablespoons very cold water

In mixing bowl, cut shortening into flour and salt with a fork. Add 1 tablespoon of water at a time, mixing with fork until all of mixture is moist. Divide dough into two parts.

Spread flour on counter and roll half of dough out in a rough circle. Place in pie pan. Pour in filling. Repeat with second half of dough and place on top of apple pie filling. Seal edges by pinching the top and bottom crusts together. Using a sharp knife, slice air vents in the top crust. Dust with ¼ teaspoon cinnamon and 1 tablespoon sugar.

Bake at 350 degrees for 60 minutes. Serves 6-8.

{Quotes from *Redemption*}

"The consequences of his year away from God had, in the end, cost him everything."

"Redemption. That was the word that kept coming up, time and time and time again. For so long he hadn't wanted to believe it, hadn't thought it possible. But now he knew with absolute certainty the truth of what Kari had showed him, what the Lord now whispered in his soul."

{Pizazz}

Go all out with an all-American picnic. Spread a red-and-white checkered cloth on your table and serve the apple pie and ice cream on matching paper plates along with fresh lemonade or hot coffee.

That's Interesting!

Karen Kingsbury also writes music and she loves to play Frisbee and Ping-Pong.

{Cracking the Spine}

Use these questions and comments to get women talking.

- Tim Jacobs chooses to ignore God's promptings. Have you experienced a time when you "heard" God? If so, how did you respond?

- When Kari's family learns of the affair and her desire to save her marriage, some of them fight against her decision. Have you ever made a decision you believed honored God, but then found that your decision was unfavorable to those closest to you? If so, how did you deal with their questions and criticisms?

- John Baxter encourages his daughter to go to church by saying, "Everyone has issues, sweetheart. Families don't get through life without a little sadness." Are you likely to find encouragement in a comment like this? Why or why not? If not, what words *would* encourage you?

- In an attempt to "help" Kari, Brooke points out, "All I'm saying is that I think the Bible gives you a way out in this case." Do you tend to agree with Brooke or Kari? What Scripture is Brooke referring to, and is she right?

- Tim Jacobs refuses to touch alcohol because of a family history of alcoholism. After leaving Kari and rejecting God, Tim finds solace in the bottle. How might sacrificing a relationship with God lead to a change of actions and attitudes? Have you seen this in your own life or the life of someone dear to you?

- Ryan struggles to right his relationship with God and with Kari. Through reading 1 Corinthians 13, Ryan realizes his love did not align with God's view of love. Take a look at 1 Corinthians 13. In what ways did Ryan's love for Kari not match up with the love talked about in Scripture?

{The Reference Section}

You may want to use these additional Bible verses during your discussion.

- Isaiah 43:1—We belong to God.

- Philippians 3:13—Forget the past and look ahead.

girlfriends
unlimited